GOD THE REDEEMER

GOD THE REDEEMER

A THEOLOGY OF THE GOSPEL

PAUL MCGLASSON

WESTMINSTER/JOHN KNOX PRESS
LOUISVILLE, KENTUCKY

Unless otherwise noted, scripture quotations are from the New Revised Standard Version of the Bible, copyright © 1989 by the Division of Christian Education of the National Council of the Churches of Christ in the U.S.A., and are used by permission.

Scripture quotations marked KJV are from the King James Version of the Bible.

Book design by Drew Stevens

First edition

Published by Westminster/John Knox Press
Louisville, Kentucky

This book is printed on acid-free paper that meets the American National Standards Institute Z39.48 standard.∞

PRINTED IN THE UNITED STATES OF AMERICA
9 8 7 6 5 4 3 2 1

Library of Congress Cataloging-in-Publication Data

McGlasson, Paul.
  God the Redeemer : a theology of the Gospel / Paul McGlasson. —
1st ed.
      p.   cm.
  Includes bibliographical references.
  ISBN 0-664-25377-6 (pbk. : alk. paper)

  1. Theology, Doctrinal. I. Title.
BT75.2.M393
230—dc20   92-13034

CONTENTS

PREFACE

WHAT DO we preach when we preach the gospel? The present work is born out of the struggle in the church to answer this question. The answer will not come from a book in theology. It will come, as it has always come, from a fresh attempt to be faithful to Holy Scripture. And it will come when and as the words of the church are words in demonstration of the Spirit and of power. The present work is written in the conviction that theology will be useful to the church when it joins with the many in the church seeking in Holy Scripture the gospel of Jesus Christ; when it abandons, that is, a position between the Bible and the church, and takes up its rightful place in the church face-to-face with Holy Scripture. The work of theology, as it is described in this book, is merely preparatory to the real work that is done daily by hosts of Christians: speaking and acting in obedience to the Word of life. If it is useful to any, may it be used for this purpose.

1

INTRODUCTION

CHRISTIANITY is on trial today, as it has always been, before the eyes of the world, seeking to legitimate its message and function in the changing contexts of culture and society. It is on trial in its own eyes as well, seeking to understand and establish its message and function amid the intramural conflicts that characterize contemporary Christian existence: Fundamentalist or liberal? Catholic or Protestant? Confessional or ecumenical? Such extra- and intramural trials are not new, however novel they may appear; they carry the Christian church along and preserve it from stagnation.

Christianity Today

THE TRIAL today of which I speak is of a different type. The stakes are infinitely higher; it is no longer a question of the well-being of the church, but of its very existence. The church is on trial with respect to the heart of its message and life. For many of us the question has become: What does the church proclaim? What breathes

life into it? What is its gospel? It is not now a question
of satisfying the serious and not-so-serious queries of
our surrounding culture, nor even of satisfying our own
serious and not-so-serious attempts at aligning and
realigning ourselves in the changing contours of church
life. It is a question now of satisfying our faith in Christ.
It is, we believe, Christ himself who tries us with *his*
question: "Who do you say that I am?"

One senses at every level of Christian life the ur-
gency of the question. It is heard in the local congrega-
tion in the hesitant yet diligent attempts to proclaim the
word of God anew. One hears it in the centers of theological scholarship and learning in the grasping for a
postmodern form of theological reflection. And one
finds the question on the lips of individual Christians
seeking to live the life of faith; it is not just a matter of
"issues" facing the Christian, but simply: "Who are we?
What do we believe? How ought we to live?"

One senses as well a readiness, even a desire, to
answer the question. The enormous resources of the
Christian church lie ready to hand—but for what?
Liturgical renewal? Ecumenical dialogue? Inner-city
mission? Yes, of course, these as well; but in, with, and
under the penultimate concerns of church life is the
ultimate concern. Whom do we preach? Whom do we
follow? Who is Jesus Christ? What is the gospel we
trust? We are ready to give account of ourselves, to be
tried and tested, whether to judgment or salvation.
Penultimate concerns can yield only a penultimate
hope, a fragmented faith, a faltering love; we seek a
Judge who, even in his severity, can offer us nothing
less than redemption of our lives.

We stand today with two thousand years of the history of Christian doctrine behind us, including generation after generation of attempts to read the Bible and proclaim the gospel. We are blessed by the richness of this history; and yet it will mean nothing to us at all if we do not act on our own responsibility to hear the word of God anew.

What resources does the Christian church today have to offer to those who would ask these questions? How is concern for the gospel present in the theology of the Christian church today? While many Christian theologies are available, there is a tendency for the language of faith in the church to separate into two religious cultures. By language of faith I mean a set of concepts and phrases by which we articulate our basic beliefs. On the one hand is the language of faith in the more liberal church; on the other hand is the language of faith in the more conservative church.[1] Each offers a basic language of faith, a basic way of speaking about the various issues the church faces. However, neither way of speaking seems to foster the kind of deep concern for the gospel that has surfaced in so many ways. Concern for the gospel is there, but where can the questions it generates be adequately asked and answered? The language of faith in the more liberal church and the language of faith in the more conservative church seem primarily designed to establish boundaries of acceptable Christian language, boundaries beyond which discussion cannot go. The boundaries are clear enough, but what about the center? What about the gospel itself? To be sure, the language of the gospel is there; but is not the primary function of that language to establish boundaries, to

11

set liberal against conservative and conservative against liberal? Is not the result of this opposition simply to close off theological discussion, and therefore to hinder a fresh and vigorous witness in the church?[2]

The Christian community today must return from its boundaries to its own center. It must return to the gospel of Jesus Christ, turn afresh to the word of God in Holy Scripture. We must seek there a new point of departure for theology and the witness of the church, a point beyond the two languages of faith in the church today.

Overinterpreting the Gospel

ON THE one hand is liberal Christianity, formulated in the context of the changing forms of "modern" theology from the post-Reformation period to the present. Liberal Christianity is faith seeking legitimation, faith seeking accountability to and status within modern secular culture. The theology of liberal Christianity seeks to interpret the meaning and truth of Christian faith by using as criteria of meaning and truth the cultural agenda of modern Western humanity. In the Enlightenment this meant faith as a series of propositional affirmations about supernatural realities, affirmations that were either identical to, or at least compatible with, the privileged representations of reason. In the nineteenth century, faith sought legitimation in the form of an appeal to a depth dimension of universal human experience—Schleiermacher's "feeling"—which is both distinguished from and yet is presupposed by and accompanies every act of human knowing and doing. In the twentieth century, modern theology found its criteria of meaning and truth in the philosophy of existentialism, the "decision" of the individual to exist in authenticity rather than being carried along in self-alienation by the objects of experience in society, technology, and the world. And more recently, modern theology has based itself on the sociopolitical discourses of self-actualization and liberation, in which self-empowerment and empowerment by God are considered correlative.

Contemporary theology certainly has as one option continuing along the lines of modern theology in an attempt to seek legitimation and a place in contemporary secular culture. Yet such a procedure raises serious questions. In the first place, liberation theologians have forcefully demonstrated that modern secular culture is in fact white, male, middle-class, Eurocentric culture, and has provided the conditions for racism, sexism, and colonial oppression. "Culture" is not a kind of universal language, but is in fact interested language. The various human activities that one groups together under such a rubric are in fact engaged in by very specific people and groups of people and often have social and economic effects far beyond the "intentions" of the original language users. When modern theology used criteria from secular culture for the interpretation of religion, it always thought it was using a privileged, indeed a universal aspect of human experience, whether "reason," or "experience," or "existence," or other familiar options in modern theology. The attempt was to build theology on the stable foundation of our modern "worldview." But such foundationalism has come crashing to the ground with the realization that one is adjusting one particular discourse (religion), not to universal human experience, but simply to another particular discourse (such as modern philosophy, science, or social theory). These other discourses are equally partial, and hardly above suspicion as providers of universal criteria of meaning and truth.[3]

Second, modern theology has failed in its original intention of providing a way of compromise and unity beyond the supposed narrow-minded conflicts of religious dogmatism. It has been argued that characteristically "modern" forms of theology arose in the seventeenth and eighteenth centuries (one thinks of Locke's *The Reasonableness of Christianity*) as a way of displacing the confessional wars—both theological and military—that characterized the new pluralism of Christianity resulting from the collapse of medieval "Christendom" during the Reformation. Where once the unitary religious world—the "orthodox" religion— had provided its own criteria of meaning and truth, now an alternative had to be sought to douse the flames generated by the competing claims of various confessional orthodoxies (such as Roman Catholic, Lutheran, or Reformed). Again, it was thought that not religion itself, but secular culture could provide the standpoint for interpretation necessary to move religion forward to a unitary, peaceful existence. Has this happened? Granting the brilliant achievements of Locke and Lessing, of Schleiermacher and Ritschl, of Bultmann and Tillich, has modern theology found the fulcrum from which the squalid and pitiable dissensions of modern "denominationalism" could be lifted to a higher place of religious unity? Or indeed—which seems more obvious in our time—has theology simply removed itself so far from the Christian faith it is trying to interpret that it no longer seems able to address the living confession of the Christian church?

No one can deny the brilliant achievement of modern theology, its lasting contribution to the discourse of Christianity. The question remains, however, whether it has ceased to function effectively in its self-described role: to appeal to the church and modern culture as an adequate interpretation of Christianity. Moreover, has it successfully solved the problem of religious pluralism and conflict created by the loss of "Christendom" and the advent of modern denominational Christianity?

Perhaps an even more difficult, yet necessary, question, however, is whether Christian language and faith have suffered at the hands of modern theology the loss of their own center. I would argue that modern theology has solved the problems of Christian belief in modern culture, not by interpreting the gospel, but by *over*interpreting it. When criteria of meaning and truth are outside the language of faith—whether the rationalism of the Enlightenment, the romanticism of the nineteenth century, or existentialism and sociopolitical discourse in the twentieth—can the language of faith speak from its own center, from within its own resources, or is it not an alien voice that one hears? The gospel must be interpreted, else it says nothing at all. But the method of interpretation—the hermeneutical theory—that has dominated characteristically modern forms of theological discourse has exhausted itself by devolving into a bewildering conflict of interpretations without a center, without a persuasive presence in modern secular culture, without any organic relation to the community of faith, and therefore without a future.

Underinterpreting the Gospel

ON THE other hand is the theology of fundamentalism, interpreting and supporting the church life of the conservative Christian communities.[4] Fundamentalism is based on the rejection of modern Western culture as the foundation for the interpretation of the meaning and truth of Christian faith. Fundamentalism identifies modern culture as "secular humanism," not with admiration or the security of self-identification, but with rejection and criticism. To be fundamentalist theologically means to reject modern secular culture. It means to reject modern scientific cosmology in favor of creationism as a scientific view of the origins of the physical universe. It means to reject evolutionary conceptions of the origin and change of natural species in favor of theistic science. It means rejection of modern ethical reasoning in favor of universal, absolute principles of right and wrong. Perhaps most comprehensively, to be fundamentalist means to reject the relativism that seems to be an ingredient in much modern culture. Truth is what it is despite the altering and faltering conceptions of it that humans attempt to attain, and as such truth is not relative, but absolute.

For this reason, fundamentalism not only rejects the modern theological project of using as criteria for the interpretation of Christian faith the changing forms of modern culture, it rejects the very notion of interpretation as a proper category for theology. Theology is not interpretation; it is an articulation of the truth. Interpretation is the attempt of human beings to conceive reality, and in this very attempt there can only be failure. To be fundamentalist means to return to the fundamentals, to reassert, that is, the great truths of the Christian faith in a religious world where those great truths have been hopelessly compromised and misconstrued at the hands of liberal theologians.

Again, it is no use denying the powerful impact and achievement of fundamentalist theology in contemporary Christian life. For some, clarity has replaced confusion, certainty replaced doubt, affirmation replaced denial. Nevertheless, it seems apparent that, like liberal theology, fundamentalist theology has exhausted its resources for building a consensus in the Christian community. In the first place, precisely as a *denial* of modernity, fundamentalism is parasitic upon modernity for its very existence. It has primarily a corrective, or combative, existence: it lives off what it rejects. It does not have a constitutive existence, depending on the center of the language of faith for the basic resources of its life. It too might lose its center, not by directly compromising Christian belief in favor of modernity, but by making the rejection of modernity—everything from rock music to modern biological science—the fundamental criterion for assessing the meaning and truth of religion.

In the second place, it is only an illusion that fundamentalism is not an "interpretation" of Christian belief, that it reads the Bible "literally," and therefore truthfully, without interpretation.[5] Indeed, precisely here is the

17

worst failing of fundamentalist theology: it *underinter-prets* the gospel, and in so doing, loses it straightaway. To believe that a "literalistic" reading of the Bible reproduces biblical truth exactly, without interpretation, has two results. It blurs the distinction between Bible and theology, thus elevating one's interpretation to the level of biblical truth, and it conceals from one the extent to which one reads into the Bible one's own culture and self-interest. Paradoxically enough, the results of such underinterpretation of the gospel are precisely the same as the liberal Christian overinterpretation of the gospel: secular cultural concerns—in this case, conservative politics, law-and-order legal systems, anticommunist foreign policy, support for the Krugerrand in South Africa, unabashed affirmation of the basic greed of much middle-class American business life—threaten to displace the Bible, and the biblical Christ, from the center. This displacement is concealed from fundamentalist theology because of the illusion of an uninterpreted truth. It is nevertheless just as apparent as in liberal theology that fundamentalism has a cultural agenda hardly derived from the Bible as its sole focus.[6]

Opening the Door

"LISTEN! I am standing at the door, knocking; if you hear my voice and open the door, I will come in to you and eat with you, and you with me" (Rev. 3:20). So says Christ to the church, and so we ask: How do we open the door? How do we invite him in? Where do we hear his voice? Nothing less than this is at stake in the question concerning a truly evangelical theology, a theology beyond the opposition between liberal and conservative traditions that dominates the contemporary discussion. The point is not at all to establish a centrist position, a Hegelian synthesis beyond thesis and antithesis. The point, rather, is to find the Center, the One who is not inside the dialectic at all, not part of the system, but who comes to us from outside precisely as the Center. Not liberal, fundamentalist—and now, "moderate"; but liberal, fundamentalist—and now, *converted*, turned around, returning to the Christ of the Bible. The question for the church today must quite simply be, *What is the gospel of Jesus Christ?*

The answer must be sought in a new theological interpretation of Holy Scripture. A new theological interpretation of Holy Scripture is necessary, first of all, in opposition to the biblical exegesis of modern theology. Modern theology has been accompanied by the brilliant development of the historical-critical method, beginning in the seventeenth century and flourishing virtually unchallenged on into the twentieth. Whether in the form of text criticism, source criticism, form criticism, redaction criticism, or sociohistorical analysis, the historical-critical method has offered an analytical approach to the biblical text that centers on the reconstruction of the literary and social development of Israel and the early Christian church. A text has meaning, in this view, insofar as it refers to, or is a function of, this historical development.

Now, to be sure, the historical-critical interpretation of biblical texts is arguably a completely separate movement in modern religion from characteristically "modern" forms of theology. Indeed, one might simply say that theology has often put historical-critical interpretation to a use that the practitioners of the method do not unanimously endorse. Nevertheless, it is clear that the historical-critical approach has prospered because it offered to theology an analysis of the Bible that (1) distanced the meaning of the biblical text from the intramural doctrinal conflicts that characterized the age of confessionalism in which it arose, and (2) tied the interpretation of the Bible together with standard, universal academic methodology. The result has been that, in both respects, with the decline of "modern" theology, the historical-critical method is losing its purpose. Communities of faith no longer find much use for a method of interpretation originally designed to distance them from their own language of faith. While it may have served an important function for a time, the historical-critical method has, much like the allegorical method that dominated medieval theology, suddenly found itself without an audience.

A new theological interpretation of scripture is likewise necessary in opposition to the "literalism" of the fundamentalist exegesis of the Bible. In literalism (similar in name only to the *sensus literalis* of Luther and Calvin), the text of scripture has meaning insofar as it embodies ideal truths in the form of logically stated doctrinal propositions (the so-called "propositional" view of revelation). These ideal truths are considered "facts" of divine revelation, to be relied on and considered as spoken by the very mouth of God. Literalism is designed precisely to combat the historical-critical method by responding apologetically to the challenge to the historical reliability, scientific accuracy, and religious purity of biblical texts. The precritical debate saw no signs of modern literalism (propositional revelation, mechanical inspiration—both antimodern ideas), but was instead characterized by the use of allegorical levels of interpretation and, during the Reformation, the tension between the allegorical sense and the literal sense. Fundamentalist interpretation of the Bible asks similar questions of the historical-critical reading; it is only the *answers* that are different: indeed, they are in opposition. Questions such as, What really happened in the life of Jesus? inspire on the one hand a reconstruction of the early history of the "Jesus movement," and on the other hand the affirmation that the facts are just as the text says they are. The text of the Bible "means" insofar as it refers truthfully, in which its "truth value" is resident in its capacity to refer to or represent facts. The Bible functions in both cases as a *source*.[7]

The literalism of fundamentalism is unsatisfying for one fundamental reason: it operates with the illusion of an uninterpreted text. To be literal supposedly means to appropriate the words of the Bible without interpretation, and thus without the misuse of the Bible that occurs in the liberal church. Fundamentalist exegesis is therefore concealed from its own interpretation: its reliance on the eighteenth-century Enlightenment notion of faith as assent to logically formed propositional revelation; its deployment of the modern notion of "factuality," and especially modern theories of historical factuality; and its elevation to the level of eternal truths of revelation the cultural views and sentiments of modern communities of readers. The questions we face in

21

Christianity today, central questions about the very meaning of the gospel of Jesus Christ, are at the same time more radical and more traditional than the scope of the literalist reading.

We need a new theological interpretation of Holy Scripture. Theological interpretation of scripture is not so much a new method (it can, in fact, be pluralistic methodologically) as it is a new *direction* for the interpretation of the Bible. Theological interpretation moves from the biblical world to the world of the reader, not vice versa. That is to say, it reverses the great Reversal (as charted in the works of Hans Frei) of early modern theology, the hermeneutical shift that occurred around the seventeenth century. Modern conceptions of history replaced biblical narrative, science replaced parable, *Weltweisheit* replaced psalm and proverb; that is, the criteria of meaning and truth in the interpretation of biblical texts were preestablished by the world of the reader. Theological interpretation means interpretation of the Bible in which the reader finds her or his way into the world of the Bible, rather than the fusion of horizons. The Bible is God's word, not ours; it establishes therefore its own criteria of meaning and truth in interpretation.

But that means that theological interpretation hears in Holy Scripture a witness to the crucified and risen Lord Jesus Christ, head of the church and savior of the world. The "strange new world" of the Bible is the shock, the surprise, the utter awe and joy of encounter with the living Lord through the power of the Spirit. Indeed, the biblical text itself does not generate a "world" for the reader; rather, Jesus Christ himself, through the power of the Spirit, speaks his word through the voices of the text. I do not mean to suggest, however, that the Spirit of Christ is to be separated from the text of scripture, for the Spirit is neither to be separated nor to be identified. The point is that truly theological interpretation of Holy Scripture follows the witness of the prophets and the apostles to the living Lord of whom they speak. The text is not a source, but a witness.

As it means a new direction, theological interpretation of scripture also means a place in which to interpret scripture. That place is the community of faith in the risen Lord as circumscribed by the canonical form and function of the Bible. The community of faith is identified by its fundamental loyalty to the witness of scripture as the *regula fidei* of its existence. It is the word of God to the church. Now, the text of the Bible can certainly be interpreted in many other ways, for example, as a source for the reconstruction of the history of Judaism and early Christianity. Nevertheless, while not denying the plurality of readings, theological interpretation means the decision to take one's place in the community of faith in Jesus Christ where the Bible functions as God's word, and means indeed the desire to hear it as God's word. Once again, theological reading does not mean an uninterpreted text, as if the reading of the Bible in the church now becomes the extended meaning of the text. Fundamentalist literalism, protestations to the contrary, often involves just such an extension of meaning through "proof texts" and the like. Theological interpretation, though always taking place in the community of faith, recognizes that more than one interpretation is offered within the community of faith as the most adequate. It also recognizes that interpretations vary over time, as indeed they should, because the God who speaks in the Bible is a living God.

To read the Bible canonically likewise means to interpret as scripture the canonical form of the Bible. Canon means much more than a list of books; it means as well the final form of the text, the form of the text shaped by Israel and the early Christian church as the decisive witness to Jesus Christ. Modern historical-critical interpretation has uncovered layers of textuality and pretextual forms of discourse that stand behind the present literary forms of the biblical books. Though this history is important in discerning the canonical shaping of the biblical witness, theological interpretation means the decision to interpret the canonical form of the books as scripture. Canon is part of the *place* of interpretation in the community of faith, because it means hearing the witness of these texts to Jesus Christ as they were spoken to us by Israel and the early church. We read these texts not *because* they were spoken thus by Israel and the church, but because, by faith, we too hear the voice of God as we read them this way.

With the insistence on the canonical form of the biblical text will come, it is hoped, a reconciliation between the scholarly study of the Bible and the general Christian reading of biblical texts. For some time now, the historical-critical study has clearly become a privileged study, that is, a mode of analysis that fundamentally alters the interdependence of text, community, and reader and places the biblical critic outside of this organic relation. Theological interpretation most certainly insists on advanced scholarly study; but it recognizes that the same text is under study as in the community of faith. The scholarly study of the Bible is then but a more critical, more disciplined, more self-conscious attempt at performing the same act of reading as the common Christian one. It is not a different act of reading altogether, with a fundamentally different text.

Theological interpretation is, finally, a *movement* of interpretation—from repentance, to expectation, in obedience. Repentance is turning around the way we think, reordering the dialectic of interpretation. The Bible is not first of all an answer to our questions. We may dig deeply into the treasure chest of our lives and find there to lay before scripture all the unanswered questions of meaning and purpose, all the unmet needs of guilt and anxiety. We come to scripture with these our questions and we ask: What will you answer? And it lies silent, or its answer is hardly noticeable. We must turn around. The Bible, as the word of God to us, questions *us*. Then it begins to speak clearly and with power. And on us falls the responsibility to give answers to its questions. Read theologically, the Bible examines us, searches us, interprets us; our act of interpretation is but an enactment of the responsibility that being questioned by the Bible entails.

Repentance in the act of interpretation is undertaken in expectation, in hopeful longing and confidence that the answer on our lips, the exegesis and theology we offer in freedom and responsibility, is fruitful witness to the word of God. Theological interpretation is not a closed circle; it is not a guaranteed method by which to move from the word of God then to the word of God now. It is an open movement of repentance and expectation because it recognizes that God alone is a fit witness of himself in his word (as Calvin stressed), and therefore that effective and obedient witness to the word of God can come only through the free gift of God. This grace of God is not method, not movement, not correlation, not divinization, not presupposition; this grace of God is the lavish and bounteous offer and promise: "Ask, and it will be given you; search, and you will find; knock, and the door will be opened for you" (Matt. 7:7). We turn to Holy Scripture expecting from it the very word of God. To expect less is to lose everything.

The movement of interpretation is undertaken in obedience. The goal of the theological interpretation of scripture is not "understanding" of the "meaning" of the Bible; the goal is new life in God as promised in the gospel of Jesus Christ. Now, new life is not lifelessness; we have hearts and wills and minds, and therefore have need and opportunity to think critically, to reflect, to question, to reason, to imagine, to feel. Obedience to what we hear in Holy Scripture does not mean blind acceptance or unreflective acquiescence to a supposedly authoritative utterance. Obedience to what we hear in the Bible, as a movement in theological interpretation, means conceding to scripture the right to establish its own criteria of meaning and truth. It is true not because we judge it to be true; we judge it to be true because it is true. Still, we must indeed judge it to be true; we must exercise all skill in discerning and evaluating the truth it speaks to us. But again, the movement is from the Bible to reader, not the reverse; it is a hand reaching out and taking hold of us, and we are free to rest easy in its grasp.

Theology has an opportunity to go beyond the conflict of interpretations that has stalemated contemporary theological discourse. The church needs a way beyond the opposition of fundamentalism and liberalism, which has played itself out in exhaustion and bitterness. But the center we seek is not somewhere concealed in the middle between left and right. Beyond all opposition and the conflict of interpretations, the Center is the gospel of Jesus Christ himself. Theology and the church can find their way out only if they begin in the Center. "Who do you say that I am?" In fear and trembling, yet in expectation and hope, we *must* give our answer to this question.

2

THE GOSPEL OF GOD

THE CHURCH lives by its confession of the gospel of
Jesus Christ. In every act of mercy, in every moment of
Christian witness in the preaching of the word, in the
celebration of the sacrament, in active solidarity with
the poor and oppressed, and in the silent prayer of the
solitary disciple, the gospel of Jesus Christ accompanies
the church, or it is not the church that acts. The church
may stutter and stammer when it speaks, but speak the
gospel it must. The gospel of Jesus Christ is therefore
the Center of the theology of the church. Theology, too,
has varied concerns: it reflects on the history of the
Christian religion, the language of faith, the theory of
interpretation; it attests the creation of God, the nature
of human existence, the destiny of human history.
Again, the gospel of Jesus Christ must accompany and
guide theology in all these concerns, or it is not theology
of the church, not Christian theology. It too may stammer and stutter as it speaks; it too may lose its way now
and then, only to find it again; but attest the gospel it
must, seek the gospel it must.

For the Christian community, the gospel of Jesus Christ is not one truth among others; it is the source of all truth, and is indeed the truth itself. In making this confession, the church is not elevating one finite human perspective to the realm of absolute truth. The Christian community is fully conscious of the intrinsic limits of all human discourse. Indeed, precisely as hearers of the gospel those in the community encourage the knowledge of these limits and studies to practice the discipline of humility in their own speech and action. The gospel is the source of all truth in the Christian community because in the gospel of Jesus Christ, God is revealed to everyone who has faith. The gospel of Jesus Christ is the gospel of God; it comes from God, manifests God, and leads back to God. Christians believe because they find God in the gospel.

In finding God, Christians find themselves. "God" is not just a final addition to human nature, not a mere item of knowledge, not the final copestone to the edifice of a mature moral personality. God is life. God transforms life. God gives new life. In confessing the gospel of Jesus Christ, Christians find their humanity defined in a new way; old definitions, however attractive and wise, are set aside and forgotten.

The gospel of Jesus Christ in the Christian community manifests God and gives life. The theology of the Christian community must not, therefore, shrink back from its responsibility to speak of this God and this life. Indeed, as Christian theology it does not want to do so, for it cannot with satisfaction hide the very source of its being. To speak the gospel is to speak of God. We must learn once again, with fear and trembling, with reverence and humility and honor, but also with joy and grace and freedom, to take this name upon our lips.[1]

The gospel is about a relationship between God and humankind, a relationship that Jesus announces as the kingdom of God. Jesus Christ announces the coming of the kingdom of God, but with the astonishing claim that *today* this is fulfilled in your hearing. In his person and work the kingdom of God has come upon you. Indeed, Jesus Christ himself is the new world of God, the Messiah of Israel. But his coming, while real, is concealed. Eyes must be opened to see his work; ears must be opened to hear his word. It is no less real in its concealment. The Messiah has indeed come. But when he comes, he calls for response: He calls for the obedience of faith.

We must be clear that when Jesus proclaims the coming of the kingdom, he is not "discussing" a new conception of God and humanity. Jesus does not use "God-talk." Rather, his word comes as shock, as surprise, as overwhelming reality and claim which I can no longer evade. And when it comes, it brings the crisis of decision.

The New World of God

WHO IS the God of the gospel? What can we believe about God? How can we find God? What does this God have to do with us? The attempt to answer these questions must begin with the simple recognition that in the gospel of Jesus Christ is a witness to God. In calling Jesus a witness we do not say everything that can be

said of him; we shall have to postpone till later speaking
of him as the presence of God, and indeed as the
response of humanity to God. But even in our all-too-
earnest desire to hasten to the mystery of the incarnation, we must not rush right past the simple fact that
Jesus Christ testifies of God, bears witness to God,
speaks of God, tells parables of God.

The witness of Jesus Christ to God uses a specific
language for its testimony; it does not invent an altogether new language. The language of the gospel is the
language of the people of Israel, the language of scripture. Jesus Christ could speak with this language what
none could say before ("You have heard that it was said
. . . . But I say to you"). Nevertheless, even in trans-
forming the language of the scripture of Israel, the point
was not to question the language so much as it was to
question the users of the language. The point is that we
who hear today the witness to God of Jesus Christ in the
gospel must decide to use this language ourselves in our
conversation with the testimony of Christ. The Jesus
Christ of the Gospels is the Jesus Christ of the whole
Bible (the "Old" and "New" Testaments), or he is not
the Jesus Christ of the Gospels. It is certainly up to us
to make sense for ourselves of the words and works of
Jesus; but the way to do that is not to translate them
into our words, so much as it is to learn the richness of
the biblical way of speaking and thinking, and that way
is to be sought in the world of the Bible as a whole.

"Jesus came to Galilee, proclaiming the good news
[gospel] of God, and saying, 'The time is fulfilled, and
the kingdom of God has come near; repent, and believe
in the good news'" (Mark 1:14–15). The first word of

the witness of Jesus Christ to God is his witness to the *basileia* of God, the "kingdom of God," or "rule of God," or, perhaps we can say, the new world of God (see Matt. 19:28). When Jesus speaks[2] to us of God he straightaway speaks of the sovereign will of God for human life, of God who defines himself and is defined for us in terms of God's will to make right the world. In that sense, Calvin was right; the primary question of the gospel is not, What is God? but, How is God toward us? The answer of the gospel is: God is God toward us in God's will for our lives.

The new world of God is new as the fulfillment of a promise, not as the replacement of something discarded. The promise that the new world of God fulfills is the covenant of God with the people of Israel. *Basileia* of God is the covenant of God enacted and fulfilled. As with the witness of Israel, the witness of Jesus Christ to God centers on the fact that God is who God is in God's desire to be with humanity, to be the God of humanity, to be in relationship to humanity.

The time has come, testifies Jesus, for God alone to be God in the world. The kingdom of God, or new world of God, is the world in which God alone is God, the world in which false gods are unmasked and dethroned. To speak of God as the "king" of humanity, or to attest the "sovereignty" of God, is not therefore to adopt and reinforce an abstract principle of hierarchy or great chain of being in which "God" is the supreme being. God is not in competition with the world, and therefore needs no victory over it. God is in competition with false gods. We are, quite simply, blinded by false gods from seeing the true God. God is there. God is ready to exercise grace and love in relationship with the human race, but we turn away, withdraw from God's presence. Let God alone be God, testifies Jesus; learn to recognize God for who God is; turn away from your turning away, and God alone will be God—the world, the new world of God has come upon you.

The will of God in the world is *blessing* (Matt. 5:1-12). When God is God in the world, we are blessed. The blessing of God is the fulfillment of the covenant of God with Israel, the relationship of God with humankind. In this relationship, God wills the good of the creature. The lame can walk again, the sick are made well; the lonely are embraced, the poor are given food and drink; the distressed are comforted, the oppressed are liberated; the blind can see, the dead are raised. God wills the good of the creature in such a way that both the creature and God are fully and completely who they are in this relationship of blessing. To embrace the new world of God means largely to *trust* the blessing that God offers as the highest good. It is a good that we cannot give ourselves, for we have traded it in for a false good, a counterfeit blessing of our own choosing. For God to be God in our lives means for us to trust the will of God for our good, which is the blessing of God.

God is God in the blessing that God offers. We can hardly hear this witness of Jesus Christ to us today. We can certainly think of our good: We can determine with precision and skill the necessary ingredients of a world in which we find the fullest of our humanity. We can "think" God; we can project our way beyond the sphere of human concern to the infinite reaches of divine being. But in the witness of Christ we hear not of such a being,

34

nor indeed of such a human good; we hear instead of a God whose being is in the relationship of blessing to humanity. We hear of a good of humanity that is only in this relationship of blessing to God. Perhaps there is an element of paradox, and certainly of mystery in this equation. Nevertheless, the most striking aspect about it is surely that it is quite simply marvelous.

What kind of relationship between God and humanity does Jesus Christ attest in the gospel of the kingdom of God? There is clearly implied a certain order in this relationship, a relation of superordination and subordination, of first and second, of leader and follower, of teacher and pupil. The history of Christian doctrine shows a tendency to reel back and forth between the extremes of this relationship—to move first to the Augustinian emphasis on divine sovereignty, divine superiority, divine ordering, divine decision, and then to react with the Arminian insistence on human disposing, human decision, human participation, human choice. However, the God of the gospel is not in competition with the fulfillment of human reality, nor is the true fulfillment of human reality set over against the reality of God. Jesus Christ attests a God whose glory is the salvation of the creature, a God whose sovereign rule over human life is exercised in the form of the gift of human freedom and the rescuing of human beings from bondage. We can hear all of this and more when we hear Jesus bear witness to God as our Father.

Here, especially, we must listen to the witness of Holy Scripture as it addresses us in our world. That God is our Father is not a projection onto "God" of our experience of fatherhood. When Jesus proclaims the God of the kingdom as Father, he first of all discloses his own identity and his relation to the God of Israel. It is not projection, but proclamation, indeed revelation; God is the Father of Jesus Christ. But, more, the radically good news of the gospel is that in the kingdom of God, God is our Father too.[3]

That God is our Father stipulates the nature of the relationship between God and humanity: it is a relation characterized first of all by familiarity, our new familiarity with God based on God's familiarity with us. We *know* God in the gospel. God is not distant, not foreign, not strange. God has drawn near us, and the word of God is on our lips and in our hearts. When we seek God in the gospel we find God, and realize in finding that God has been seeking us. God is God in this "search for humanity." Now, to be sure, we are estranged from God by our own rebellion; but we are not estranged in such a way that a final veil of ignorance has descended over the human race, enacting and confirming once for all a final wall of separation between finite and infinite, creature and creator. Despite our rebellion, God has turned toward us and draws near. The nearness of God is not a violation of the boundaries of the human—it is indeed an establishment and protection of those boundaries. The fatherhood of God is not the enslavement of his children but the protection of his children from enslavement to self and others.

Precisely in God's familiarity to us God is disclosed in mystery, as mystery. This only seems paradoxical, insofar as mystery has come to mean to us nothing but incomprehensibility, as if the mystery of God is a kind of property of God whereby God is always just beyond our grasp. However, in the gospel of Jesus mystery is not primarily the unknown; mystery is that which is known only from God and to God. From God—genuine knowledge of God in the gospel is knowledge given by God and comes only as the gift of God's grace. Such knowing is a human act, using human intellect and will, and resulting in human experience; but it does not derive from human capacity, nor can it be appropriately assessed from the critical standpoint of human experience and self-definition. I know God, and in knowing know that it is not I who know, but God who knows me. I will God, and in willing I realize that it is not I who will, but God who wills me. I desire God, and in desiring feel that it is not I who desire, but God who desires me.

And to God—in knowing and willing God I do not exercise one option among others, one particular use of my human resources as distinguished from others. I know, rather, with what Martin Buber calls the power of exclusivity: God alone is the object of my knowledge, God alone the source and goal of my strength and will and desire. To know the God of the gospel of Jesus Christ is to say yes to the one truth of my life, a truth I do not discover for myself; nor can I evade it or protect it among other truths. This knowledge is entirely vulnerable to its object. I cannot control it, even for the sake of keeping it constant. To will God does not mean to choose among alternatives; it means, rather, to experience the freedom of the gospel of God. Any other "choice" is no choice at all in the light of the gospel. I do not come to the gospel with freedom; I find my freedom in the gospel and exercise it only as freedom for God.

The mystery of God is therefore the nature of God's knowability, rather than the incomprehensibility of God. God is mystery precisely in the knowledge of God. Attempts, ancient and modern, to assert conceptually the incomprehensibility of God do not seem to do full justice to the Christian doctrine of divine mystery. They may be interesting reflections on the intrinsic limits of human reasoning and experience, but the mystery of God is a confession about God, not a self-limitation of the human.

We are led by these reflections on the God of the gospel to the confession of the election of God. The God of the gospel creates hearers of the gospel. Jesus testifies to the God of the gospel in such a way as to make clear that this God is not one among other life options; one cannot simply turn to God as one may turn to other sources of meaning and comfort in this life. One cannot turn to God at all, if by this is meant the exercise of resources and capacities that exist for the purpose of human self-definition and self-actualization. In the gospel of Christ, and in the announcement of the coming of the new world of God, God has turned to us; as hearers of the gospel we are those to whom God has turned, those to whom God has drawn near. From beginning to end the coming of the kingdom of God is a divine act of grace and mercy.

What does this mean? What can it mean to those of us who have seen the rise and fall of the doctrine of predestination, with its obviously treacherous impact on some periods and some movements of Christianity? To be sure, the unattractive and historically troublesome aspects of a point of view are not infallible tests of its truth or falsity. Nevertheless, we hear the word of the gospel in the community of faith, not as isolated propositional truths. In the community of faith it is difficult not to sense the uneasiness bred of years of scorn and neglect heaped upon this doctrine. But we cannot simply close our ears to the word of Christ: "All things have been handed over to me by my Father; and no one knows the Son except the Father, and no one knows the Father except the Son and anyone to whom the Son chooses to reveal him" (Matt. 11:27).

The God of the gospel creates hearers of the gospel, creates followers of God. In bearing witness to God, Jesus can thus preach the gospel only in such a way as to exclude the illusion that we can make ourselves hearers of the gospel, make ourselves followers of God. The gospel of Jesus must exclude even as it includes. Indeed, it must exclude precisely in order to include. The gospel of God comes to us as the grace of God's election or it does not come to us at all. We are left with only one option: simple trust. We are free to trust that God has indeed drawn near to bridge the chasm of sin and evil. Without this simple trust we can only take offense. As Kierkegaard argued, the option of offense is itself only an illusory option; in taking it, we sense ourselves exercising the right of judgment concerning the truth of the gospel, whereas in fact the truth of the gospel of God is exercising its right of judgment over us. But this right of judgment is for the sake of the divine right of acceptance and grace: Jesus offers to us the testimony that God will not finally accept the self-defeat of the human and the loss of the divine. Where we are without resources, God chooses us. "Come to me, all you that are weary and are carrying heavy burdens, and I will give you rest. Take my yoke upon you, and learn from me; for I am gentle and humble in heart, and you will find rest for your souls. For my yoke is easy, and my burden is light" (Matt. 11:28-30).

The election of God in the gospel is not only my sense that I choose God because I have been chosen by God; it also means that God has chosen relationship to humanity as the final and victorious word about our lives. Jesus Christ is himself the sign of this divine commitment; indeed, Jesus Christ *is* this divine commitment, in that God has, in him, taken this commitment as far as it can go. Where humankind have corrupted and denied this relation to God with abandon, God has remained faithful to his choice. God chose us in love to be his children through Jesus Christ, according to the purpose of his will.

We must now consider a further question concerning the gospel of the kingdom: Can God still be God and be in relationship with another? Even as king over us, is he not to some extent delimited by us, if we are seriously to believe that he exists in relationship with us? In answer to this question, we must turn to the biblical concept of the righteousness of God.

Here we must first notice a difficulty. We are accustomed to understanding the righteousness of God as somehow different from, indeed opposed to, the gospel. The righteousness of God, we say, belongs to a different sphere of divine truth—the law—and is entirely alien to the gospel of love and mercy. It may be necessary for Christians to confess the righteousness of God, but certainly not in the same breath as they celebrate the gospel of Christ. Now, the problem with this under-standing is that the Bible clearly says that the righteous-ness of God is revealed in the gospel (Rom. 1:16–17)! If we fail to see God's righteousness here in the gospel of Jesus Christ, we fail to see it at all.

The righteousness of God is God's life, God's charac-ter. It is certainly not a standard of behavior by which God is judged: there are no standards of righteousness independent of God; still less is anyone in a position to apply them to him in judgment. God is righteous because God is righteousness; that is, God is always God—God lives and acts in the character of his own eternal being.

It is in this sense, then, that God's righteousness is involved in the proclamation of the gospel of the king-dom. God is always God, even in relationship to another that is not God. God both originates and conducts the relationship in such a way that God is eternally consis-tent with himself. On the one hand, this means the intimate involvement of God. God invests his very char-acter in pursuing this relationship with humanity. Nothing less than who he is as God is put on the line in his willing and enacting relationship to us. On the other hand, this means the freedom of God. God can commit himself to us without being compromised by us. How-soever we act toward God, he will always be righteous to us.

Knowing the righteousness of God is therefore our confidence that we are dealing with God in the gospel of the kingdom. He will not give us less than himself. If we have trust in the righteousness of God, we know that the kingdom of God is not some kind of drama, not a performance of a God who in himself is different from the part he plays. At the same time, the righteousness of God means our fear of God. In the gospel of the kingdom there can be no polite agreement with God to relax for the time being the strictness of the rules of the game. There are no rules, and indeed there is no game. God is God, or he is nothing. We are in relationship to him as he is, or we are reaching out into the void.

Finally, the righteousness of God is not only who God is, it is a gift that he gives to another. All that is not God comes from God, as God's creation. In any relationship, each partner to some extent comes to share the character of the other. How much more so in this relationship, in which the other is dependent on God for its very existence! God is righteous, and he wills to make this righteousness the character of the world that he has made. Now, in becoming righteous the world certainly does not become God. The world does come, however, to reflect in its own creaturely way the character of God. A righteous world is a world that bears the stamp of its creator. One hears of such a world and reflects: Yes, this is the kind of world such a God would create and sustain! If we are to become children of God in the new world of the kingdom, his righteousness must become real in our lives as his gift to us.

God is righteous in all his ways; he is always God, and his being cannot be compromised. If this is so, can God really be affected by a reality outside himself? Can it matter to God, really matter, what happens to his creatures? If he is God without us, can he really be God *with* us? Does God care?

We must again begin our reflections by noticing a difficulty. Since patristic theology it has been customary in

Christian doctrine to speak of divine "impassibility," that is, the inability of God truly to be affected by reality outside himself. To "suffer" the effects of another on oneself is to change. And according to the Neoplatonic conceptuality of medieval thought, to change is to be corruptible. If God is pure, incorruptible being, God cannot change; therefore God cannot be affected by reality outside himself. While the conceptuality is now different—the Neoplatonic chain of being giving way to the Newtonian world of causality—the modern theistic conception of God often shares the same characteristic, the same "imprisonment in his own eternity" (Barth). We now seem to have an opportunity for fresh theological reflection on the biblical witness to God.[4]

The gospel of Jesus Christ proclaims that God's very identity is bound up with his relationship to his creatures. Our welfare affects who God is. He rejoices when the lost are saved; he is angry when sin and evil oppress and destroy us; he is patient when we persist in our sloth and pride; he tenderly and lovingly nurtures us when we fall behind. God cares about human life. To be sure, he is still God, still righteous in all his ways, even when we are not whole; but even as God, he suffers with us the lack of that wholeness which he wills for us.

According to the gospel, God cares especially for the human wholeness that is lost through oppression and affliction. He cares for the poor who suffer degradation and deprivation at the hands of the rich, and for the outcast and homeless, those whom society has pushed aside. God cares for those who have abused themselves, for "tax collectors, prostitutes, and sinners," for those of us who, for one reason or another, traded away our whole human reality for broken and fragmented lives. He cares for the sick and dying, for the mentally disabled, for those whom drugs have destroyed.

But we speak in generalities. God cares, according to the gospel, for the individual, for each of us. Every tear, every slip in life, every moment of anxiety and panic, every night of pain and loneliness, every act of weakness and sin, every listless hour of boredom and directionless waiting, affects God. It matters to God that I become all that I can be, as an individual different from every other individual. It matters to God that forces of sin and evil have a power over my life, a power to corrupt and destroy and vanquish. It matters to God that I die, that I come to be and, through death, experience in my person the final destructive power of evil.

Yet, what does it mean to say that God cares about these things? The gospel of Jesus Christ proclaims that God cares about them, and the picture is not complete until we come to speak of the death and resurrection of Jesus for our sake. The fact is that no theory, no doctrine, no theology can successfully conceptualize what needs to be known here. Theology can bear witness and point to this reality, but the reality must finally speak for itself to everyone that hears, every eye that sees. God cares. Far beyond our ability to think and speak, God cares. Believe it.

God with Humanity

"WHO DO YOU say that I am?" In seeking to understand the gospel of God, we are led ineluctably to the question of the identity of the One who proclaims it. The gospel of God speaks to us, we have seen, a message that we cannot speak to ourselves, and it challenges and invites its hearers with sovereign freedom and grace. The One who brings this message must be like us, or else he could not communicate with us, could not bring home to our lives the content of the gospel. But he must likewise be unlike us, for we look around us in vain for anyone who could with persuasion deliver to us such a message. Indeed, he who speaks of God to those who have faith in this way must himself be of God. As Peter himself confessed, "You are the Christ, the Son of the living God" (see Matt. 16:16).

Jesus Christ is the Son of God; this alone can be the content of our confession. We must make clear to ourselves that in making this confession we are taking on our shoulders a responsibility: we are accepting the responsibility of giving an answer to the question of Christ, "Who do you say that I am?" Many called him Christ who failed in this confession. Many claim him Lord who know him not. Many indeed hailed him as Son of God, Messiah, yet delivered him to be crucified. We today who call him Son of God are not free, therefore, simply to repeat their words as if that alone discharges our obligation.

The point is not to look to ourselves to find our own values with which to ascribe importance and uniqueness to Jesus of Nazareth. Jesus without exception rejects the ascriptions of values and religious affirmations of others in the New Testament, no matter how exalted and impressive. The point, rather, is precisely to cease relying on our own resources to understand and affirm the identity of this person. Only his own self-description is adequate; but his self-description is not a logically closed circle—it leaves open the question of how we might take it onto *our* lips, how indeed for us also it might be true that Jesus Christ is the Son of God.

In the language of the Gospel of John, Jesus is the Son of God sent by the Father. The Bible can speak this way about God, here as elsewhere in the Gospel story, because by "Father," "Son," and "Spirit" it does not mean three images of God or expressions of God. The theological dynamic of the Gospel story is lost entirely if one imagines that "God" is somehow behind the triune name of God and the story in which this name is embedded. We can, like the Bible itself, use "God" language, and "Father, Son, and Spirit" language; but precisely in doing so we must realize that we are addressing the same reality.

God is identified for us in the Bible as Father, Son, and Spirit, one God, who lives eternally and acts in this unity in difference. As we tell the Gospel story, we shall see this God act for us to redeem our lives; we shall see Father, Son, and Spirit act on our behalf in their unity in difference, in their mutual relation to and distinction from one another. The Father sends the Son to save, the Son whom he loves eternally as his own. The Son is sent by the Father, loved eternally by the Father and "close to the Father's heart" (John 1:18). The Spirit "comes from the Father" (John 15:26), and is the Spirit of the Son, the bond of love in the eternal life of God. God is who he is in this eternal self-relation. This is the God of the gospel, the God who turns to us in redeeming love.

The biblical witness to Jesus Christ everywhere confesses the identity of the earthly Jesus and the eternal

Son of God. Jesus Christ is God incarnate. It further-more assumes the identity of the earthly Jesus and the exalted Lord of the resurrection. Indeed, it is the risen Lord, calling forth resurrection faith, who manifests to the eyes of faith the identity of the earthly Jesus. This basic biblical witness, grounded in the self-revelation of the risen Lord Jesus Christ, is echoed in countless ways in the creeds, confessions, hymns, and liturgy of the church. If theology today is to recover its role in the lan-guage of faith, it too must be grounded in the basic con-fession of the gospel.

The biblical witnesses also everywhere proclaim that the eternal Son of God, in becoming incarnate, hum-bled himself, becoming obedient unto death. The mys-tery of the incarnation is the self-humiliation of God, for this is the way in which God saves the world. As with the kingdom of God, so with the coming of the Son of God; his coming is real, but real in concealment. To those of faith, the kingdom has come, the Son of God has appeared; to those who doubt, there is nothing but offense and blasphemy. In coming in this way, Jesus Christ presses us to decision; and in coming in this way, Jesus Christ seals his fate as the crucified Messiah of Israel and savior of the world.

While the Gospels are agreed on this basic christolog-ical confession of the Christian faith, they offer a rich and manifold witness to the movement of God into our space and time in redemption of the world. We shall speak below of Jesus of Nazareth as the "presence" of God and the "power" of God. The point, however, is not to offer a closed christological system. Rather, these theological reflections on the Gospel witness are offered as an invitation to renewed theological study of the biblical witness to Jesus Christ, in service of the ongoing task of fresh proclamation of his name in the church and to the world.

God is present with us in Jesus Christ. This presence of God fulfills a promise that stretches back to the beginning of time, that functions indeed as the very purpose of God's history with the human race. To Abraham, to Isaac, to Jacob; to Moses and the people of Israel; to David, to Isaiah; to the people of Israel in captivity—God promises to be with God's children. The presence of God means first of all the intimate relationship of creator and creature. Likewise it means the relationship of forgiveness between the righteous and the unrighteous. It is, in fact, the final fulfillment of the purpose of human life—to be in unity with the very God who made us, with the One who is far above all that we can think, all that we can seek, all that we can hope for and dream. The presence of God in Jesus Christ may thus be new as the fulfillment of this promise; but precisely as the fulfillment of the promise it is not unexpected. Like Anna and Simeon, those awaiting the coming of God find in Jesus Christ the one final answer of God.

Jesus Christ is the Son of God, truly God and truly human. He is not a third thing, floating somewhere between divinity and humanity; he is the Mediator, the One in whom divinity has condescended to humanity in order to redeem it. As the Mediator, Jesus Christ defines for us true divinity and true humanity. We do not, or should not, arrive at the judgment that Jesus is the Son of God with preconceived notions of divinity and humanity, even supposedly Christian ones. The first commandment for Christians is that such preconceived notions are in fact idols—even the supposedly Christian, or religious, notions—in light of the true Mediator of God and humanity. We may heap our notions of the divine onto Christ, only to have them cast back by the One who said, "I never knew you." We may lavish our ideas of ideal humanity onto Christ, only to have them exposed for what they are: attempts at self-justification. Jesus defines God and humanity to us or he is not the Son of God.

To know the presence of God in Jesus means to have in him one's Lord. To have Jesus as the Lord of one's life means to abolish the claims of other lords. Jesus never manifested his own divinity without acting to rescue human beings from the hold of false gods over their lives. The Christian church of our age is in danger of losing the knowledge of the divinity of Jesus Christ, for we so often combine the Lordship of Jesus Christ with the false gods of the world. In the name of Christ we link God and country; we juxtapose the name of Christ with every conceivable human cause and ideology; through the false notion that they are "blessing," we accept as divine grants wealth, status, privilege; we elevate our political and cultural agendas to this divine status. These are idols. They are terrible signs that the deity of Jesus Christ is celebrated only in name among those who refuse to find their God in him and in no other. Jesus Christ is God; Jesus therefore defines "God," because only God can define himself. Put into the equations by which we elevate our own concerns to the level of the divine, even the "deity" of Jesus becomes in our hearts the idol of our own making. We lose him.

It is central to the Gospel story that when the disciples come to confess Jesus as the Christ, the Son of the living God, Jesus discloses to them the purpose of his coming. He came to suffer and die for our sins, to be crucified on the cross for the salvation of the world. And it is also significant for us that the disciples immediately react with horror. This cannot be! The Son of God must reign in power! He has chosen us to reign with him! But this misunderstanding Jesus can only rebuke in sharpest language: "Get behind me, Satan!" Here surely is the word of Christ that we must hear. To have Jesus as the Lord of one's life means to follow his way: the way of denying oneself, taking up the cross, and following him. The point is not self-denial as a new ideology; the point, rather, is living fellowship with the crucified Lord as the end to all ideology. Self-empowerment is not the way of the gospel.

What does it mean, more precisely, that Jesus is the Son of God, that God is present in this man, Jesus of Nazareth? We cannot isolate a divine aspect of the character of Jesus of Nazareth—the unitary narrative of the New Testament does not seem to allow this—nor does it seem necessary or useful to invent a new category for describing the divine in Jesus conceptually. We can, however, make clear to ourselves, and make clear in our confession of the gospel, that when we hear and tell the story of Jesus we are hearing and telling the story of God. The word of Jesus is the word of God. The work of Jesus is the work of God. As Christians, we do not begin with the figure of Jesus and work our way back to a divinity behind or apart from him. God, we believe, has in fact worked his way among us in this human life. Jesus defines God for us because Jesus is God to us.

Jesus preached, we have seen, the kingdom of God—a new world in which God's will is affirmed for the blessing of all humankind. We are now in a position to affirm that Jesus is in fact the enacted will of God. The purpose of God the Father is fulfilled and manifested in him. Jesus Christ, attested for us in Holy Scripture and believed in by the community of faith, is the kingdom of God, the unique and definitive enactment of the will of God. He is this, first of all, because he manifests the will of God. His birth, life, death, and resurrection from the dead are a fulfillment of all righteousness, a complete picture of the will of God in human life. Secondly, Jesus enacts God's will by carrying it over and carrying it out in the finite and sinful conditions of human life. "The Word became flesh." The will of God sought, not only a showing in human life, but a direct act in one human life. The act of Jesus of Nazareth is the act of God. Who God is, and how God is toward us, is not different from who Jesus is, and how he is toward us—whether in mercy or judgment, love or rejection. Everywhere in the New Testament Jesus speaks and acts out of this unity with God. To believe in Jesus as the Son of God means to see and to recognize the complete unity of the story of Jesus and the story of God with human life, and indeed with one's own life.

Why did God become present among humankind in this man Jesus of Nazareth? What is the purpose of the incarnation? We shall not have our full consideration of this question until we consider later the cross and the resurrection; but we must now say that the assumption of human flesh by the Son of God in Jesus of Nazareth is not at all a sheer act of caprice, a religious fancy cast up

51

by the folk-poetizing of the ancient world. The element of caprice and the bizarre are encountered only when one begins one's reflection on the incarnation with pre-defined concepts of divinity and humanity that then must, in some unheard-of fashion, be brought together. Now, to be sure, it is not that in Jesus Christ the distinction between divinity and humanity is blurred; everywhere the Bible and the Christian community confess that Jesus Christ is truly God *and* truly human, not some *tertium quid*, or demiurge, combining elements of both. Nevertheless, allowing Jesus Christ to define for us both divinity and humanity, and thus beginning our reflection on the incarnation with the unity of God and humankind in his person and work, it is clear that, far from being an absurdity, the incarnation is the fulfillment of the divine purpose in all creation, the covenant between God and humankind. Jesus Christ is the fulfilled relationship between God and humanity. When the Son of God assumes human flesh, he comes to his own (John 1:1–18); he establishes and enacts the true and proper relationship between every human person and the God who is our creator and redeemer.

The embodiment of the will of God in this human life is the sign of the purpose of God in every human life. As the prologue of the Gospel of John in particular confesses, there is no "God" behind or above this enacted will; nor is there a purpose to human existence above or after this unity between God and humankind. Every other god is an idol that the Word of God shatters. Every other purpose to human life is darkness in this light from above. When we are up against Jesus of Nazareth we are not dealing with "religious" issues and concerns; we cannot find a category of questions to which he is the answer. We are dealing with God and the self; we are encountering the Lord of life and the meaning of life. How we answer to him, whether in faith or offense, is how we answer to God and how we define our existence. If we run from him, from the grace he offers and the love he commands, then we run from God and pervert our lives. If we embrace him, we know God and find our lives.

As the Son of God, Jesus Christ is the truth of God and the truth of humanity. We cannot make this confession lightly; we cannot ignore the doubts and suspicion that others will have, and that we ourselves will have even as we make it. Note the real point of the confession: *He* is the truth, not ourselves, nor even our attempts at confessing him. Christians cannot and must not convert this confidence in Christ into a self-confidence in their own ability to perceive and articulate "the truth." To confess Jesus Christ as the Son of God means to accept the inherent limits of human ways of experiencing the world and seeking the truth, for it means to accept that the criteria of meaning and truth are in this person, not in the language of human culture—including the language of the Christian religion in abstraction from its living content. Christian belief is "eccentric"; it is centered outside itself, and therefore content to admit its own transparency to Christ in a world culture of relativism. Faith in Christ means trust in him as the truth, not trust that we possess the truth in our perceiving and knowing him.

Yet we live in a culture, largely secularized and certainly thoroughly pluralistic. How can we say that in this

one human being the truth of God and the truth of
humanity are present? Of the hundreds of competing
claims to truth, competing interpretations of the world,
competing systems of value, why this truth? this interpretation? this value? There are those who have
stressed the uncomfortable "fit" of Christianity with
Western culture to the point of making it a systematic
truth of faith. Whether as "the absurd," or "the paradox," or simply "mystery," for these theologians the
complete clash of Christ and culture is a necessary
aspect of embracing the truth of Christ. Is not such a
view in its own way a concealed confidence in human
culture? Does it not make the truth of Christ the opposite, or perhaps the limit, of human understanding, but
for that very reason dependent on human understanding for its meaning and truth? When we have reached
the limits of human understanding by contradicting its
structure and scope in the paradox, what have we
reached but the limits of human understanding? Have
we therefore reached Christ? No; to find the truth of
God in Jesus Christ is neither a confirmation of the languages of human culture nor a contradiction of them.
This finding cannot be converted into any aspect of
human culture; it is a finding that can only be sought
again and again in him.

Jesus is not only the presence of God; he is also the
power of God. The words and works of Jesus Christ are
full of wonder because they are the words and works of
the Son of God. His words appeal to no authority beyond
himself for legitimation: they are words of power, his
power. His works, too, are full of power: he heals those
who are sick, gives sight to the blind, restores speech

and hearing to those who are without them. He raises the dead. At his command, the forces of darkness flee from their perversion and destruction of human life.

Jesus Christ lives among us, and offers himself to us, as One whose life is filled with the power of God. But what kind of acts are these, the so-called miracles of Jesus? And what kind of power do they manifest? As we have seen, Jesus both proclaims and lives the kingdom of God. He proclaims the unity of God and humanity in the new world of God; and in his life he is this new unity that he proclaims and offers to those who follow him. The words and works of Jesus are therefore words and works in the kingdom of God; they are events that, though transpiring in the space and time of the world in which we live, are events of divine-human unity which manifest the coming kingdom. They are signs of the kingdom of God which Jesus proclaims and lives. They are not themselves the kingdom: the unity of God and humanity proclaimed and lived by Jesus Christ is the kingdom of God. Nevertheless, though signs of the kingdom, Jesus' words and works participate in the reality of the kingdom. Those who are healed in faith are indeed brought near to the kingdom of God; those who are freed from the tyranny of evil forces are indeed freed for a new faith in God.

These signs of the kingdom that Jesus performs reveal to us the power of God. They identify for us the nature and purpose of divine power. We may speculate endlessly concerning the meaning and logic of divine "omnipotence," but the signs of power in the gospel of Christ truly manifest the power of God. God has and exercises the almighty power of a redeemer, of One who is the enemy of all evil. God wills to save human beings from that which tyrannizes and corrupts the good life for which they were created. Where death, sin, and the forces of evil have stolen away the fullness of human life, God the Redeemer is powerful to heal, to save, to restore. Those whom Jesus heals in faith are brought into the sphere of this redemption of God. Again, these acts of Jesus are not themselves the divine redemption; they are signs of the redemption that Jesus proclaims and lives, events in our world that signify the new world of the kingdom of God in which God and humanity are united.

In speaking of the miracles of Jesus as signs of the coming kingdom of God, we are implicitly criticizing an older view of miracle, a view that found its natural place in the worldview of modern European culture. In this view, a miracle is a "supernatural" breach in the natural order of things, a temporary lapse or disjunction in the sequence of causality which, by God's creative hand, governs the universe. Some have referred to this as the two-story view of miracle because of its clear conception of the dual structure of the universe in natural and supernatural (or finite and infinite or visible and invisible) realms. The point is not so much to find fault with such a conception; it had its merit, and to some extent was a necessary protest against the rising materialism of the Newtonian world. The point, rather, is to press on to a confession of Christ which better attests what we read and hear in Holy Scripture.

Clearly enough, the Bible has no conception of a "natural" order of things comparable to the modern view. Such a conception is only possible under the conditions of modern empirical science, which, as everyone knows, were entirely lacking in the ancient world. Just as clearly, therefore, the Bible can have no definite conception of a supernatural breach in the chain of causality. Again, the conditions for such a view are simply lacking. What is not as clear, however, is that the Bible does not speak of miracle in some prescientific worldview either—the world of magic, or the numinous. While there may be elements of an ancient, prescientific worldview in the background of the biblical witness—just as modern readers could find there some elements of the modern conception of causal order—such elements do not play a major role in the biblical testimony. For example, were the biblical witness primarily interested in the miraculous as an aspect of ancient religious culture, one central concern would surely be the careful description of how to perform the miraculous—how to reproduce a miracle—in the lives of the followers of this sacred tradition. There would be careful descriptions of incantations and rites designed to initiate the faithful into the miraculous acts. However, readers of the Bible have long been aware that, contrary to expectation, it makes no effort to transmit the legacy of the miraculous to future generations in this way.

The Bible attests "miracle" in a particular theological confession concerning the identity of Jesus Christ. The powerful words and deeds of Jesus are signs that in him the coming kingdom of God has already dawned. The Bible is not concerned with two dimensions of the universe, a natural and a supernatural, but with two *ages*, the present evil age and the age to come. The miracles of the Bible are signs in our evil age of the redemption of God in the age to come, which has come upon us in Jesus Christ.

The purpose of a miracle is to make broken lives whole, and so to engender faith. Yet so often in the Bible those who witness the coming kingdom of God in Jesus lack faith. "You of little faith," says Jesus to his disciples and to the crowds who follow him without understanding. What kind of faith do they lack? Are they simply incredulous—unwilling to believe that such things can be done, even by the Messiah? Are they unwilling to concede that the known order of things must on occasion yield to a higher law, a greater force? No, it is not credulity that Jesus requires of those whom he heals. What the followers of Jesus lack is faith in the sense of expectation; they do not expect anything from God. The immediacies of the world around them have lulled them into forgetfulness of the power of God over human life. The evil of the world around them has suppressed any sense of the goodness of God. They expect God to be neither good nor powerful, and they therefore get what they expect.

To have faith in God is to expect from God nothing less than what he promises. The gospel of Christ proclaims that God offers the kingdom of God—a new world in which the full blessing of God is present in every human life. A "miracle" in the life of this Christ is simply a sign of the final fulfillment of this promise. We believe in the God of miracles when we too expect from God what he promises. Indeed, the true miracle is that, in this expectation, we shall receive from God far more than we can hope or imagine. God is good, and his goodness rules in every human life; believe that, and you will grasp hold of the coming kingdom of God.

Perhaps the greatest sign of the mystery of Christ is the miracle of Christmas. Jesus of Nazareth was born of

Mary, who was promised in marriage to Joseph, the son of Jacob. With his birth, a new life story began, in the midst of the innumerable life stories that begin each day; but this life story was to continue and bring to fulfillment a story that began with the beginning of human history itself—the story of God's redeeming love for the human race. This was Adam's son; he was Abraham's son; he was with us, but chosen to be for us.

His was a special birth, full of wonder. It was expected, as all births are expected; but even prior to the expectation, this birth was announced by God. The angel of God promised Mary the birth of a son who would redeem the people. Others before her had heard similar promises; there were, for example, Sarah and Hannah. But Mary was a virgin, she had no family, she was not yet married; it was not yet time for her to have children. It is certainly Mary who will have a son, but he belongs to no man. According to the angel, the child comes from God. It was "conceived . . . from the Holy Spirit"—not as though God were the male parent of the child, but to make clear that the child will have no male parent. By God's power and grace, the child comes from Mary alone. The birth of this child, Jesus, of Mary the Virgin is a sign that God is present in this human life. It is not itself the reality: the Bible nowhere says that Jesus is God because he was born of a virgin. Rather, Jesus was born under this sign because he is God, because he comes from God. It is a sign that participates in the reality that it signifies. Even as she gives birth to the Redeemer, Mary shares in the joy of redemption:

> "My soul magnifies the Lord,
>   and my spirit rejoices in God my Savior,

for he has looked with favor on the lowliness
    of his servant.
  Surely, from now on all generations will
    call me blessed;
for the Mighty One has done great things
    for me,
    and holy is his name.
His mercy is for those who fear him
    from generation to generation.
He has shown strength with his arm;
    he has scattered the proud in
      the thoughts of their hearts.
He has brought down the powerful from their
      thrones,
    and lifted up the lowly;
he has filled the hungry with good things,
    and sent the rich away empty.
He has helped his servant Israel,
    in remembrance of his mercy,
according to the promise he made to our ancestors,
    to Abraham and to his descendants forever."

(Luke 1:46–55)

The Redeemer came to save those who stand in need of redemption. Even in his birth, God sets aside as a sign of this redemption one who is herself in need of help from God. He likewise "sets aside"—this time not as a sign, but as an unnecessary intrusion—all those who might share in the making of this event. There is no father of this child, only a mother. From the very beginning of this life we are forced to recognize that there is help from no other save God.

The birth of Jesus Christ is the birth of God in the world. Every other miracle of Christ is included in this miracle—that Jesus was born of a virgin, in order to attest to us that this man lives the life of God among us.

We have no category for this sign: it is not about birth in general, nor about human beginnings, nor indeed is it about the human love that was surely manifest in this birth event. Neither is it about the sexuality that was absent from this event; the cult of virginity associated with Christmas is pagan, and entirely unrelated to Jesus Christ. To see this event as the sign of the coming of God into the world, we must look where it points. We must direct our gaze with the Wise Men to an insignificant village and an insignificant family, where One is born for whom all the treasures of the world are not rich enough. We must look up with the shepherds in the fields watching the flocks and see all the creatures of God singing in praise at the news of this birth. We must open our ears to the word of God, and hear the good news of peace on earth. And even as we wonder, we must remind ourselves that this sign is not about wonder itself. This sign points to the reality that in Jesus Christ, God has entered our space, and our time, in order to redeem the world.

It is the reality signified that gives its truth to the sign, rather than the sign giving truth to the reality. Similarly, it is the fulfillment that gives its truth to the promise, rather than the promise giving truth to the fulfillment. There is nothing about a virgin birth, nor indeed about the other events involved in the birth of Jesus Christ, that contributes in any way to the truth that in him God was made a human being. The various attempts to improve on the biblical testimony by sundry theories concerning the biological aspects of the virgin birth—as if, for example, the absence of a father guarantees the absence of transmission of original sin, or sinful human nature—are quite simply human attempts to turn the sign into a human truth, no matter how supernatural they may sound. The virgin birth does not make Jesus divine; nor does the fulfillment of the promise make this event true. This is to confuse the sign with the thing itself. We cannot "believe in" the virgin birth, nor "believe in" the fulfillment of prophecy; we can believe in Jesus Christ, who was born of a virgin, and came into this world for our sake.

Can we have the reality apart from the sign? Can we believe in Jesus Christ and not find him as attested by the sign of his birth—the miracle of Christmas? To be sure, the virgin birth has wrongly been converted into an article of faith in such a way that it has come to take the place of the reality, as if belief that Jesus was born of a virgin is believing in Jesus as the Son of God and Savior. This confusion has likewise been exacerbated at the hands of those for whom theology is antimodern apologetic, in which belief in the virgin birth is a test of one's willingness to stand against the encroachments of modernity into Christian belief. For these reasons, the biblical testimony has been lost in the sea of liberal and conservative controversy.

Nonetheless, we can only come to admit, surely, that *we have no Christ* apart from the sign of his birth—the miracle of Christmas. Eliminate from the New Testament witness the miracle of the birth of Jesus, and indeed the miracles of his life, death, and resurrection, and one is left with no Christ at all. The miracles of Christ are in fact signs that Christ is offered to us only in a decision: faith or offense. We are certainly free and called on to interpret Christ as he is attested in scripture; but there can be no valid interpretation apart from this decision.

Jesus Christ was born of the Virgin Mary, just as surely as he suffered under Pontius Pilate, was crucified, dead, and buried. To believe in this birth is to believe that God in Christ came to rescue the lost, to redeem those who have nothing to offer in return but faith and thanksgiving. With Mary, our sister, we marvel at his coming!

Humanity with God

JESUS CHRIST is not only the presence of God in human life; he is also the true response of human life to God. Jesus Christ is true humanity; his birth, life, death, and resurrection from the dead—the story of his earthly life—define for those who believe in him the very meaning of human personhood. This may seem a simpler affair than the presumably more "arcane" elements of the traditional doctrine of the incarnation of God. In other words, that Jesus is the Son of God may appear on the surface a greater stumbling block than the fact that he is also human, the "Son of Man." But appearances deceive. In claiming true humanity for himself, the gospel of Jesus Christ will not let us rest even where we appear to ourselves most comfortable, most competent, most in control. To believe that Jesus defines true humanity is, in its own way, a greater offense to faith than believing that he defines what is truly divine. Yet believe we can and must; for the humanity that Jesus is and offers to us is inseparably part of the grace of the gospel of God.

Jesus loved God. It is with the simplicity of this statement that we can best characterize the most prominent feature of the humanity that Jesus exhibited. Jesus lived the life of one who fully loves God. He himself called it the greatest commandment: to love God with all one's heart, body, soul, and mind.

If we listen to the Gospel story, we are not led to the secret recesses of Jesus' inner life—for example, to the "consciousness" of Jesus behind his acts, or to his "intentionality"—to find his love for God. The acts of Jesus that constitute the story of Jesus' life are not outward expressions of something inside Jesus that we must discover. Instead, the acts of Jesus are the identity of Jesus; the acts of Jesus define the true humanity of Jesus. Jesus' love for God is simply the concrete and unhesitating obedience to God that characterizes the story of his life. Jesus lived the will of God, and in so doing loved God.

Now, this is not to deny that there is an "inside" and an "outside" to human experience, and to Jesus' experience in particular. According to the Bible, it is certainly possible for one to act on the outside in a way that fundamentally contradicts what one feels on the inside. This is called hypocrisy. It is not possible to feel on the inside a love for God that is only indirectly or intermittently expressed outwardly as obedience. In true love for God, inside and outside are in complete agreement, every act is a felt act, and every feeling is enacted. Both act and feeling are responses to the command of God.

Jesus' love for God is expressed in the fact that his identity is entirely a function of his relation to the proclamation of the gospel of the kingdom. There are

no rivals for the final meaning and purpose of his life—
no rival, that is, to the meaning and purpose given to it
by the calling of God. It is well known that "lives" of
Jesus have often tried to supply different aspects to
Jesus' life. He has, for example, been tied to the land of
Palestine, leaving behind the urban civilization of Jerusalem for the rustic environment of the Sea of Galilee
and the untutored, uncultured peasants. To him has
been accredited a fierce loyalty to his people, his nation,
his community. Some have ascribed to him the "traditional values" of family life. He has of course most often
been described as an intensely religious man. And,
more recently, he has been pictured as a revolutionary
agitator, struggling for the liberation of the oppressed.
Yet the New Testament is conspicuously, even notori-
ously, silent in all these ways. Jesus loves God and
therefore rejects all other claims on his life.

We can put it in the positive mode by saying that
Jesus depends on God for everything. He is entirely
exposed to God, entirely vulnerable to God's will for
his life. His entire worth comes from the voice of
God's approval—"This is my Son, the Beloved." It is
quite clear that at every turn Jesus is faced with alternative means of self-worth—and always decisively
rejects them. Instead there is a loving trust of the
worth that God gives, even in circumstances in which
the meaning and purpose of life seem contrary to the
very promises of God. "Yet, not my will but yours be
done," says Jesus in the Garden of Gethsemane (Luke
22:42). Here indeed is a love for God that conquers all
fear, even in the midst of the greatest suffering and
hopelessness.

Jesus likewise expresses his love for God in the form of zeal for God's honor and glory, a zeal that sets itself against especially human religiosity or piety. Jesus loves God and therefore hates religiosity. The practice of religion conceals the name of God under the rubble of human pride. It is only on the surface that love for God and the practice of religion are held together. The practice of religion takes the things of God, the reality and power of the rule of God, and converts them into human possessions, into opportunities for human self-aggrandizement. In Jesus' message, and in Jesus' life as well, a decision is thrust upon us: Will faith become an opportunity for true love for God, or an opportunity for enhancement of the self? Jesus' life exhibits with brilliant clarity the choice of love for God. At every turn, he chooses the path that leads to the glorification of God and leads away from the enhancement of self. He declines opportunities for religious display in his own life, in everything from the simple prayers that he offers to the company he keeps to the almost willful down-playing of his own mission. He likewise attacks the religiosity of others. The gospel of Christ is not about religion, nor is the life of Jesus a particularly religious life. It is instead about a love for God which, like a mirror, is of itself empty, only to be filled entirely by the image that it reflects.

Nothing is more obvious in Christian language than the fact that Jesus loved others, and yet nothing is less clear to us than just how true this is. We frequently hear his words about turning the other cheek, about the prodigal son and the good samaritan. Yet we seldom reflect on the fantastic reach of compassion in the story of his life. In the Gospels, Jesus' life is interwoven with the stories of countless individuals. In every case, Jesus has compassion on those whose lives intersect with his own. Universal love for humanity is simply not the point here, nor do the Gospels make use of such a concept. Jesus' love is the compassion of engagement with other individual lives.

What is the source of this compassion? What is the energy moving this human being to love others? Jesus loves others because he sees them as God sees them. His love for others is energized by his love for God. This means, first of all, this compassion for others is built on the forgiveness of sins and the possibility of new life in the kingdom of God. People move in and out of Jesus' life who have reached the end of the road of estrangement from God. Some are socially recognized as sinners, like tax collectors and prostitutes. Others sin in concealment, like the scribe and the Pharisee. Still others are estranged through ignorance of the will of God, like the Roman centurion. Jesus always sees others as God sees them, as people for whom life has become unmanageable given their own resources, but for whom wholly new life is possible through the power of God. Jesus offers no universal rule of behavior; to one he pronounces a word of conflict, to another a command to follow, to yet another a warning to change. In each instance Jesus faces the person with the reality of the old life and the possibility of the new life. He also brings to that person the key to the door from the one life to the other: forgiveness of sins.

Jesus sees others as God sees them in that he looks to the heart, not to the categories of human prejudice.

Gender, race, class have no part in the way Jesus sees others. Or, better, Jesus purposefully ignores such forms of human exclusion. Women are not "feminine"; Romans are not "the enemy"; the poor are not "those people"; in Jesus' compassionate engagement with others the absence of such perspectives is itself a silent witness to the protest by Jesus against oppression.

Finally, Jesus sees others as God sees them, and is therefore willing to suffer loss to himself for the sake of others. Now, one certainly does not get the impression of a cult of martyrdom in Jesus' life with others. The martyr, or indeed the Messiah as typically defined, sees his own death as in itself redemptive for others. The martyr suffers not so much for others as he does for himself. That is, he suffers and dies as the final fulfillment of his own life. The other simply becomes the opportunity for self-fulfillment. Jesus gives himself for others, not as a final act of self-fulfillment, but as a testimony to the fact that the self cannot fulfill itself, but can only be fulfilled by the power of God. He suffers for others as a servant, not a martyr. His focus is not on himself—indeed, he "loses" himself—but on the will of God, and on the others whom God loves and wills that he should love. Love for the other does not function to complete Jesus' personality, or to fulfill any need in Jesus' life; it is in fact the one thing needful.

Jesus lives the life of a free human being. If we would know true freedom, we can learn its meaning from the story of Jesus in the Gospels. As in so many other aspects of Christian discourse, our culture offers to Christian reflection an alternative meaning of the concept of freedom. This concept, like so many others, is a product of the brilliant flowering of Western Enlightenment philosophy. Indeed, both fundamentalism and liberalism have articulated their theologies of freedom by using this Western concept—the liberal view a version of free individual expression, the fundamentalist view a version of capitalist economics. It is time to question whether either has seen what is to be seen in the gospel of freedom.

Jesus is free in that he rejects the tyranny of definition by others. From the beginning of the Gospels to the end, people try to define Jesus' life for him. He is put into one category after another as a means of giving some meaning and purpose to his life. He is a loyal son who must protect the interests and reputation of the family. He is a teacher of wisdom, able to solve a riddle and dispense insight to the thoughtful. He is a legal scholar versed in the dialectics of Jewish doctrine. He is a revolutionary ready to cut off Roman rule and establish a rejuvenated Davidic monarchy. He is a faith healer able to display enormous feats of magic. All are to some extent true; and yet Jesus everywhere and always rejects these attempts to ascribe meaning and purpose to his life. Why? Because the Gospels picture Jesus as a name, not a category. He is free to be himself, unencumbered by preconceived ideas of identity. The fantastically rich and powerful social world of meaning available in a category comes crashing to the ground around Jesus' feet.

Does this mean that the freedom of Jesus is a self-conferred freedom? If meaning and purpose do not come from others, do they come from himself? No; Jesus likewise exhibits freedom as a rejection of the tyranny of self-definition. One looks in vain in the Gospels for the signs of a human being whose primary meaning and purpose in life are an expression of self-fulfillment. This is all the more remarkable in light of the resources that were available to Jesus, according to the Gospel picture. If ever there was a human being strong enough and wise enough to define himself as the final act of freedom, this was the one. Nevertheless, says Jesus, his will is to do the will of the One who sent him.

Jesus is free because he accepts the will of God in his life. It is God's definition of his life that gives freedom. He lives, according to the Gospel of John, as One sent by God; as One for whom a path of meaning and purpose is paved by God himself. Now, it is of course because God defines his life that he is not tyrannized by others or self. That is the negative meaning of his true freedom. But what is the positive meaning? What does it finally mean to say that Jesus is free in God? Jesus is free in that his every act is fruitful for the kingdom of God. To be free means to live one's life in the empowerment of the new world of God. The new world is not just a distant shore that beckons us. According to Jesus, and indeed as evidenced in his life, the "kingdom of heaven has come near"; it liberates its members from the tyranny of the old world and energizes them for fruitful service in the new. The freedom of Jesus is a self empowered by God and connected with others in the life of the new world of God.

The humanity of Jesus Christ is, finally, expressed in the way that he faced temptation by evil. It is not "human" to have a propensity to commit evil that must be overcome. When Jesus faces temptation, he is not confronted by his own weakness but by the power of the evil one. It is human, truly human, to face the power of the evil one through the greater power of the divine Spirit, calling on the Word of promise for deliverance.

How was Jesus tempted? He was tempted first of all by the seductive lure of the flesh, the elements of pleasure and comfort that can overcome the self and tear it away from God. Not only in the wilderness, but also throughout his life as narrated in the Gospels, Jesus is faced with the challenge rightfully to lay claim to a measure of personal fulfillment that his calling seems to deny. Not only is such fulfillment rightfully his, it is likewise his by virtue of his power to acquire it. Jesus faces the temptation of the evil one who offers him the pleasure of the flesh by trusting instead the greater pleasure and comfort of the divine word. Unlike the children of Israel in their wilderness, and unlike the world in its headlong pursuit of riches and comfort and success, this free human being chose faith rather than pleasure.

Second, Jesus was tempted by the evil one in the form of idolatry. Granted that one more powerful than himself must be worshiped for the sake of the kingdom, why must this one be the God of Israel? Why might it not be the one who already holds sway over the kingdom of this world? The elements of power and control over the world are already in place; a kingdom has already been built; why not simply assume the place of rightful heir in the kingdom by pledging allegiance to its ruler? Again, as a true human being Jesus resists the false promise of this pseudo-king. He is not after a kingdom for its own sake; he is after the kingdom of God.

Jesus will not succumb to the allure of power in and of itself. Power in and of itself, sheer ideological power, is the evil one. The almighty power of God is self-defined power, power for the sake of the rule of his righteousness and love. All other power, however successful it may appear in the world, and however able it is to build, organize, and sustain a kingdom, is of the evil one.

Third, Jesus was tempted by the evil one to misconstrue and abuse the promise of God. God has promised to be with those who fear and love him above all things. Why not use this promise to one's own advantage? The promise is there; only a fool would allow it to remain unused. If God wants to enrich and protect us, to deliver us from any harm, who are we to reject his bounty? However, according to the choices that Jesus makes in the wilderness, and makes again and again throughout his life, the promise of God came with a purpose: to extend the reach of God's rule in the world rather than the well-being of one's self. To claim the promise of God for another purpose is to "tempt God," that is, seemingly to force God into a position of acting in a way inconsistent with his own basic purpose.

The temptation of Christ is, of course, a model for our own effort to face the lure of evil, but it is much more than that. It is primarily a way for us to identify who Jesus is. That is, it first of all tells us about him, not about us or who we ought to be. Who is he as a human being? He is the very first participant in the new world of God. He is the pioneer of our faith, the discoverer of a new world. He is tempted because he leaves the old world behind even though it continues to offer him its own form of meaning and purpose. Jesus chose the new;

he is the first human being, the true Adam, who through his decision for God transforms and elevates humanity to its divinely willed meaning and purpose.

Biblical Texts for Consideration

The New World of God

Genesis 12:1–3
Deuteronomy 4:32–40
Isaiah 61
Jeremiah 31:31–34
Matthew 5–7
Mark 4
Luke 4:16–30

God with Humanity

Matthew 8
Luke 1–2
John 1:1–18
John 17
Colossians 1:15–20

Humanity with God

Matthew 9:35–38
Mark 3:1–6
Luke 4:1–13
John 15
Philippians 2:1–11

3

THE HUMAN REVOLT

THE PROCLAMATION of the gospel of the kingdom of God brings to light a new world, a world in which human beings reach the final and complete fulfillment of their lives in the divine blessing, and in which God brings to conclusion his purpose in creating a world independent of himself. In the new world of God, God and humanity are bound in relationship together; they share a relationship in which God is still free to be who he is in his righteousness and yet likewise free to be affected by the world he has made. The gospel of the kingdom furthermore proclaims that this new world of God has indeed dawned, that Jesus Christ is the Center of this world, the One in whom God has turned to humanity and in whom humanity has turned to God. Jesus is the kingdom of God enacted and fulfilled.

The gospel of the kingdom also exposes a reality very different from the new world of God in Jesus Christ. It exposes a world in which God's rule is rejected, in which relationship between God and humanity is

disrupted and mocked; a world in which human fulfillment is perverted and corrupted until only a fleeting
semblance of humanity is left to God's creatures. This
is the world of human sin. Human sinning certainly
involves the breaking of divine commandments. Yet the
moralism of much Christian preaching is but a distant
echo of the biblical testimony to human rebellion
against God. We know when we have broken rules of
behavior; then we know, or think we know, the reality
of human sin. However, in Holy Scripture sin is not
something that we can know about ourselves, not something that we are capable of discerning through self-
examination. Sin is something that comes to clarity only
in the refracted light of the new world of God's kingdom. The world of human sinning is exposed as the old
world which the new world overtakes and destroys. We
certainly experience the old world of sin even prior to
the coming of the new. We are indeed held captive by
its cunning and power. But we do not "know" what we
experience. We do not experience our own experience
until we are liberated by the gospel of Jesus Christ to
the new world of God. Then sin becomes that which we
are leaving behind, that which God has already effectively replaced with his new creation.

What does the new world of God in the gospel tell us
about the reality of human sin? It tells us first of all that,
whereas the new world of God is a world in which God
is God, in which God rules the creation he has made,
the old world of human sin is a world in which that creation is in revolt. The creature rises up against the
Creator. The creature rejects the goodness of the divine
blessing, usurping the right of blessing themselves, with

the result that the relationship between God and humanity is rejected. Again, where the new world of God offers a world in which the rights of the creature are protected and the life of the creature is nourished, the old world of human sinning is exposed as a world in which creature attacks creature, in which true relationship among God's creatures is overturned through the oppressive use of power. Finally, where the new world of God offers a world in which God's righteousness and God's care redound to the acceptance and justification of the creature, the old world of human sinning is exposed as a world in which God's righteousness and care can and must judge, and condemn, and destroy. The old world of human sinning is a rebellious assault on the goodness of God and a tearing apart of the very fabric of the universe that he has made.

Sin and Guilt

WHAT IS this old world of human sinning that has been exposed by the proclamation of the kingdom of God? Who is the human being who is caught up and overpowered by this old world? Who is the sinner?

The sinner is first of all the one who fails to recognize, acknowledge, and accept God as God. The proclamation of the rule of God in human life goes forth, but somehow the sinner misses the point. He or she hears the word of God, but fails to trace that word to its origin in God. Instead, the sinner substitutes idols, "beings that by nature are not gods" (Gal. 4:8), upon whom to fix the desire for meaning and purpose in life. Sin is first of all a disruption in divine-human relationship through human idolatry, human failure to let God be God in one's life.

What makes an idol an idol? If the Bible claims that we are all fundamentally ignorant of God, then is not every god of human imagination necessarily an idol? How is one to distinguish an idol from the true God? The familiar options for answering this question fall short of the biblical witness. God, it is said, is spirit rather than flesh; God is infinite rather than finite; God is transcendent rather than mundane; or God is eternal rather than temporal. While these conceptual distinctions may be useful in some contexts in Christian doctrine, they fail to attest and clarify what needs to be pointed out here. Indeed, such distinctions can and do foster a kind of religious idolatry, which flourishes often in the very heart of Christian language and piety. The distinction between God and an idol cannot be made conceptually, using human conceptual resources, for the simple reason that every such distinction is itself a result of human attempts to determine and fix "God," and therefore an act of human idolatry. To let God be God means to relinquish the attempt to distinguish God and an idol as an act of human knowledge. It means, instead, to recognize and affirm that knowledge of the true God is not itself the product of human knowledge but of divine revelation. When, and only when, God makes himself known in the revelation of his name is the distinction between God and an idol truly made. We can simply confess that God alone has made that distinction for us.

What light is shed on the sinner when God makes himself known as he is? It becomes clear that human beings desire a god over whom they can have some control. There are fundamentally two realities in the universe: God, and the things that God has made. Without God, the things of the universe are nothing. Without the things of the universe, God is still God. To that extent, then, God is in no way beholden to the universe of things. Quite the contrary—the universe of things is entirely beholden to God. This is just what the idolater fails to recognize and accept. The idolater realizes that as long as the self is limited to the world of things, the self can enter into a relationship of codependency with its idols. Codependency—when one provides the condition for the possibility of the other, and vice versa—brings with it a measure of control, control by the self over its idol. At the same time, however, it brings with it a certain amount of control by the idol over the self!

Indeed, such is the perverse irony of idolatry exposed by the gospel: although the self can find limited freedom in serving an idol, it eventually finds itself consumed by the need of the idol to exercise its own terrible freedom. And the self finds itself in bondage. Addiction to drugs, for example, exercises just such a terrible dialectic in the human heart. Who can fathom the idols of our age? The political gods who promise what they cannot deliver? The social gods who steal away the hearts and minds of people? The gods of pleasure and riches that hold captive the seemingly good people who serve them? Our problem is certainly not "secular humanism." Would that our society were even more secular, even more humanistic, even more content to find within the universe of people and things nothing but people and things, and not a god. Ours, rather, is an age in which the world of idols has broken free of any restraint, terrorizing the earth with the innocent lure of an outstretched hand and the pummeling force of a clenched fist.

Furthermore, the sinner is the one who will not, or cannot, trust the goodness of God. The old world of human sinning is a world in which the goodness of God is ignored or derided. To mistrust God means no longer to expect from God the promised fulfillment of one's life. According to the gospel of the kingdom, the rule of God in human life brings with it the final and complete fulfillment of the good of the creature. God exercises his righteousness and care by establishing, nourishing, and protecting the life of those whom he has made. The sinner is the one who, on hearing this gospel of divine goodness, mistrusts the goodness of the divine offer.

Now we are accustomed, unfortunately, to portraying mistrust of God as theoretical doubt concerning the existence of God. That is, we mistake mistrust for skepticism, as if the problem of our age is an inability to convince ourselves and others that one such as God truly exists. Skeptical doubt is not itself the real problem; it has, rather, all the characteristics of the rationalization of a far deeper, more significant feature of our experience. Our real problem is that we cannot and will not expect to receive from God the good that he promises. Mistrust is a failure of expectation, not a lack of cognitive assent.

Why? Why do we fail to expect from God the good that he offers? The consequences are no less than devastating; the very meaning and purpose of our existence is at stake. Why do we draw back? Certainly the Bible has a great deal to say about this, and we shall analyze more fully in the pages ahead its portrayal of human pride, selfishness, and sloth. Fundamentally, the testimony of scripture is that human beings mistrust God for no reason at all. It is a meaningless and irrational act, imbued perhaps with all sorts of motives and significance, but fundamentally in itself without any cause or purpose. It is not even fair to say that we fail to expect good from God because we arrogate to ourselves the privilege of defining and enacting our own good. We certainly do that, as we shall see; but it is a result, rather than a cause, of a mistrust of divine bounty.

Because it lacks any real reason and purpose, the old world of mistrust of God is a world turned upside down, a chaotic world spinning off into the void with no center, no direction. It is not really even a world—if by that we mean an ordered, and to some extent successfully functioning, universe. Mistrust of God is not a principle on which to build an ordered life; it is, rather, the black hole of a disintegrated self. In that sense, to mistrust God is not a human choice. Choice presupposes a self capable of rationally distinguishing and deciding between alternatives. In mistrust of God, the self relinquishes its hold on the good and ordered world of divine creation in favor of a chaotic and meaningless universe. It is driven; it does not choose. Neither can it opt out; it must indeed be rescued.

Through idolatry and mistrust the sinner is a rebel against the kingdom of God and is driven by the power of the old world. The self in revolt is a self that loses its connectedness to God as the fulfillment of its being. Without the connectedness, it is supremely isolated, yet it must continue to exist in a world of other people and things, and indeed is continually reminded that it must continue to exist with God, against God. But how? Shorn of its connectedness, of its relatedness, how can it find its fulfillment?

On the one hand, the self can continue to exist in a world of other people and things and can continue to negotiate a relationship to God through pride. The proud sinner is the sinner who breaks out of the isolation of the self by finding the self wherever he or she looks in the world of people and things, and in the very face of God. In pride, the self resolves all things into itself. Relationships with people, or the mere semblance of them that is possible here, become opportunities for self-enhancement. We "manage" our relationships to others based on the criterion of personal growth—and, of course, in doing so never really see others at all. In pride, the world of things—the world of material, social, political culture—becomes a mirror for the self, a place for the self to find reflected its own image. Here, image is everything; the self is no longer able to see things for what they are, but only for what they offer in terms of self-reflection. The tragic consumerism of our society, from which no one is immune, is built on the proud sinner in the world of things.

Finally, the self in its pride tries to bridge the chasm between God and the self through the projection of the self onto eternity. It need not technically worship itself to fall prey to pride in relationship to God; it need only appropriate to itself the right of final and definitive fulfillment. Such a person is unwilling, and perhaps unable, to receive the gift of meaning and purpose in life from another. This self sees only two alternatives:

either I define myself, and then fulfill my life; or I am defined by someone else, and therefore am subject to the superior strength of another. Such a person is no longer aware of the possibility of fulfillment in relation to another, and especially in relation to the Lord of life. Proud of his or her achievement, and defiant in opposition to all perceived forms of authoritarian religion, the sinner in revolt looks for and finds a god to whom nothing is owed and from whom all can be expected.

On the other hand, the sinner can respond to the disruption of the relationship between the self and God through an attempt to lose the self altogether in apathy or carelessness or sloth. The slothful sinner too is aware that he or she must continue to live in a world of people and things, and also is reminded continually of the claim of God on human life. The slothful sinner can make a kind of peace in the self by simply allowing it to merge outward into the world; walls of identity come sliding down until the self is merely a flicker of light in a forest fire.

The slothful self needs take no responsibility for life, for it is carried along without resistance by the stream of things. While for the proud sinner the world is a mirror, the slothful person is a mirror to the world. He or she seeks only to be what is expected, only to reflect back to others the image that will meet the least disapproval. This fosters the illusion of a kind of concern for others, and a certain level of relatedness to others based on this concern, whereas in fact there is no relatedness at all, but only the desperate need to avoid being a self in relation.

The slothful sinner cannot be sure if there is a God, and even if there is, is not altogether sure what to do about it. He or she knows that there might be something to belief in God, since so many confess that they have it; but to insist on organized religion as the place where this God might be found and worshiped is going much too far. Better a "supreme being," a "spirit" who lives in us all and to some extent protects our lives from harm. The slothful sinner may pray when in danger and worship on nationally sanctioned holy days, but "God" is otherwise seldom considered. Moved by trends of fashion and taste, by intellectual and emotional symbols of widest appeal, the slothful sinner, much like the proud sinner, is easy prey to the ravages of consumerism, for whom the reality of the living God is the worst possible threat.

Finally, the sinner is the hypocrite, the one who conceals his or her sin behind a veil of religious devotion. Being a religious person may seem to be the most appropriate way to live in the kingdom of God. However, in the New Testament, Jesus condemns the most religious people—the Pharisees—as the worst sinners of all. Why? Certainly, one reason is the sheer pretense of such religiosity. It offers acts of charity rather than a charitable heart; devotional exercises rather than a heart open to God; obedience to the commandments, rather than love of the law and the Lawgiver. The hypocrite is a rebel in the new world of God's rule, but seeks to hide rebellion by outward show of allegiance to the new order. Yet God sees all, God in Christ exposes all and judges not the outward show but the inward disposition. The hypocrite, for all the tragedy of life, finally comes across almost comically. It is foolish to pretend.

Hypocrisy as a sin means more than simple pretense. Hypocrisy is religion as a kind of controlled experiment, where we do what we do only to the extent that we have some measure of control over the circumstance and meaning of our action. It is a self-determined world of religious meaning and truth—self-determined, and therefore manipulable. Do we need to be more righteous? Then we can support justice and peace in the world. Do we need to love God more? Then we can learn to worship with more liturgical awareness and sophistication. Do we need clearer knowledge of the divine will? Then we can turn to the Bible more often to find confirmation of our basic insights into the divine. For the hypocrite, religion is a way within the control of the self to "fix" the self and its problems. Faith becomes my "spiritual journey"; it is a therapy that strikes the hypocrite as perhaps the best, and certainly a useful, way to the fundamental happiness the person craves.

Why is the hypocrite so roundly condemned by Jesus in the Gospels? Why is it upon the hypocrite that Jesus pronounces the great woe reminiscent of the prophets of Israel? As a hypocrite, I think I am inside the kingdom of God, and may indeed have a glimmer of what it all means. I am for that reason all the more accountable when I act the sinner. My sin is to embrace the world of religion rather than embracing God and my neighbor. Because I seize on religion as a therapy within my control, I simply cannot imagine the glory of God, which is so far beyond my control. Because I act religiously to protect my own interests, I do not have a clue to the reality and need of my neighbor, the man or woman who crosses my path. I pray, I read the Bible, I attend church, I proclaim the creed, but I know not God, nor the justice, the mercy, the love of God. The hypocrite fundamentally hates what cannot be controlled—without control there is no self-preservation. What the hypocrite does not see is that God is precisely that which we cannot control, the One who, in power and glory, is far above all our ability to manipulate the world of things and persons. Strangely enough, this uncontrollable God is the only hope for our preservation.

Affliction and Oppression

WE HAVE considered, so far, sin as a disruption in the relationship between God and the creature, as a revolt of the creature against the God of the new world. What we must now consider is the effect of this revolt on the creature itself. That is, we must observe the creature existing in the old world of sin and rebellion, side by side with others in the same dire straits. To put it differently, we have so far focused on the vertical dimension of sin; we must now consider the horizontal dimension. Both are crucial dimensions in the biblical witness, much as love for God and love for neighbor are the First and Second Commandments, inextricably linked. But, though linked, they are different; and we are only now in a position to observe the disordered and chaotic world of the sinner—now that we have discovered the secret of the sinner in his or her rebellion against God.

The New Testament speaks of this sinner, estranged from God, as held captive by the power of the flesh.

The term "flesh" does not mean the physical body per se, though the body can be involved. Rather, "flesh" refers to the power of sin and evil corrupting and perverting the human self. The flesh is the self in bondage to sin and evil. The integrity of the human person is lost, to be replaced by the disintegrated and counterfeit humanity of the flesh. Or again, to use another biblical concept, the sinner in estrangement from God is held in bondage to the power of lust. Without God, the self must complete itself—but with what? It ranges the world over for the source of its fulfillment, and cannot rest until something comes to fill up the measure of its emptiness. The self is addicted—to addiction, to the desire for something to satisfy its desire. In the name of freedom and personal fulfillment, the self in sin gives itself over to the desperate and anxious search for definitive fulfillment.

It turns to things—not things in general, but things that it can make its own, possessions. Jesus called this desire to possess the love of "mammon," and points out that it and love for God are mutually exclusive. The church in American culture can only lament, and indeed repent grievously, at the effects of such greed on our lives and the oftentimes willing participation of the church in this terrible scourge. Whether or not those are right who portray America as the home of capitalistic avarice—though perhaps our national culture once stood for so much more—the fact remains that greed is not only a sin, it is a destructive power over the self which drives it away from openness to the new world of God. At issue here is not the right to private property, or indeed market economics versus socialist economics;

such issues belong to legalists and economists. At issue is the presence of God in human life, and the terrible *no* to God that results where people are held captive by possessions. The materialism of our culture is wrong, and is destroying lives. Inward detachment from things is not enough.

Again, the self in bondage to the flesh can turn to sexual pleasure, what the New Testament calls "lust" or "perversion." The self turns to other human beings, not other human beings in general, but as bodies which the self can possess. Lust is a turning of the self to the body of another in order to find in its embrace the fulfillment of life that is lacking. It is an endless quest, an endless search, a bottomless pit of desire. It is not at all like the sexuality depicted in the Bible—the giving and receiving of pleasure between married lovers. Too often the conservative churches have confused lust with sexuality and have adopted a thoroughly pagan antipathy to sexual pleasure. Lust is to sexuality what mammon is to the gift of food and drink and clothing from God. Ours is a culture that is absolutely ravaged by the destructive power of lust.

The self in bondage to the flesh can also turn to alcohol and drugs to fill up the hole in the middle of our life without God. There is no denying that many factors account for the problem of substance abuse in our time—social, economic, psychological, and so forth. That recognition does not minimize the destructive power of substance abuse; it only means that such social, political, and psychological forces are themselves part of the sin and evil of our culture, from the racism that produces our urban ghettos, to the militarism that diverts our national resources from the elimination of poverty, to the corporate culture that has caused and legitimated much alcoholism and drug abuse. Our culture, which gives rise to addiction, is corrupt; but the bondage of the self to drugs and alcohol is not for that reason neutral, a mere function of a larger system of cause and effect. The person who turns to alcohol and drugs is giving away the self to bondage.

The sinner is held captive by desire, and therefore must have what he or she wants. And to get the object of desire, the sinner must take it from another. The sinner must forcefully extract from the other what is considered to be his or her due. The result is a fundamental distortion of the human relationality disclosed in the gospel of the kingdom. Instead of the relationship of justice and kindness and love between human beings commanded by God, there is oppression.

Oppression is the abuse of another, especially the poor, the marginalized, the vulnerable. Men abuse women, physically and emotionally; we live in a culture of sexual harassment, of rape, of violence against women. Whites abuse people of color; ours is a culture of continuing racism and bigotry and prejudice, often making use of the tool of economic violence. Rich take their due from the poor; in our culture of economic violence, the rich get richer and the poor get poorer. Wealthy nations abuse poor nations, putting economic gain above human rights in international relations. Adults abuse children, perhaps the most vulnerable of all. The abuse of the vulnerable in these ways is an affront against the God who is our creator and redeemer. It violates God's special embrace and invitation to the poor, for in Jesus Christ, God knows what it means to be vulnerable.

With oppression comes injustice, the failure to protect the rights of everyone, especially the weak and marginalized. The old world of sin is a world in which the weak are at the mercy of the strong. Despite the relative efforts of some political systems, the minor successes of some legal systems, the attempts of some economic systems, injustice remains an everyday experience for the vast majority of human beings living in the world. The fragmented relationship to God that occurs in sin results in the terrible fragmentation of relationships between human beings. After millennia of human cultural experiments, we still find ourselves unable to protect the rights of others at even the most fundamental levels.

Injustice breeds violence. Where the rights of others are not protected—at least not effectively—the other becomes simply another object in the way of our own personal self-fulfillment. I respond to the other as a thing, not as a person. Whatever form it takes, violence is always the final result of a chain reaction that begins with the evil desires of the heart, giving rise to oppression and injustice and yielding finally a personal and social existence in which violence becomes an almost necessary ingredient.

What can we do? We can throw up our hands in helpless resignation, recognizing the superior power of sin and evil and the limits of the human ability to withstand it. We can make an island of relative security for ourselves, perhaps also for our family and friends. We can shore up whatever walls of protection we can find to withstand the assault of the proud and oppressive sinners who would use our loss for their gain. But then what have we done? Have we not too simply entered willy-nilly into the circle of violence and injustice and oppression? Have we not, too, begun to treat other persons and things as something to be either protected as our own or released into the ownership of someone else? The sad fact is that helpless resignation in the face of oppression is itself one way of joining the forces of oppression.

Or we can take a more active approach, with eyes open joining the forces of oppression. We can become people who hate: people who hate those of another color, who hate those of the other gender, who hate the poor and the weak. We can learn to hate anyone who stands in the way of our getting what we want, as well as anyone who by existing reminds us of what we have become. To be sure, our society has slowly made such hatred a less acceptable, and in many cases illegal, form of human relatedness. Laws alone are not strong enough to conquer the force of hatred as it is passed from person to person and generation to generation.

Finally, we can take an approach that is far less realistic than the response either of resignation or of willing participation in oppression. In fact, it is a response that is built on an illusion, the illusion of innocence. That is, we can respond to the sin of humanity by taking on the role of the world's judge. We can become experts at noticing, analyzing, and cataloging the ways in which human beings threaten and harm one another. We can learn to apply the wisdom we gain to individual cases, perhaps volunteering our service on occasion to instruct the wayward. Our response to the evil of the world is to point out how wrong it is.

Why is this approach so illusory? Why does Jesus make those who act as judge against sin seem to be worse than those whom they are judging? First of all, the judge falsely assumes a relationship of innocence toward the neighbor. If I proclaim you guilty, I am, at least by implication, proclaiming myself innocent. It is precisely this self-ascribed innocence that I claim gives me the right to act as judge. To assume that I am innocent in a world of sin and evil is ipso facto to fail to recognize the power and extent of that sin and evil. The act of judging another is a self-defeating position, in that it assumes for myself a position of innocence I cannot possibly have if my judgment against others is true—if, that is, it truthfully bears witness to the extent and power of sin and evil in the world.

More importantly, by judging another I assume for myself a certain stance in relationship with God. That is, I assume for myself the wisdom and judgment needed to apply the rule of divine justice. But divine justice is nothing but the will of God, which is simply God himself—his command to the creature. By judging another, I assume for myself the right to measure the world against God, and therefore, by implication, the ability to measure God against the world. Now we are back to the beginning of our reflections on sin, for a god whom I can measure is an idol. The idolater and the judge are one and the same. Neither can the judge escape the power and extent of sin in the world; in fact, in his or her own way, the judge is the final logical outcome of all human sinning.

The Judgment of God

THE GOSPEL of Jesus Christ not only exposes to view the nature and extent of the human revolt against the will of God in human life, it likewise attests to the divine reaction to human sinning. Jesus lays before each human life a choice: the embracing of the new world of God brought near in his life, or the refusal to participate in the new world because of the lure of sin. There is no neutral humanity, no human being who lives some-where beyond or apart from this choice. The proclama-tion of the gospel excludes the possibility of such a neutral humanity. Whether we say with Jesus, "Who-ever is not with me is against me," or "Whoever is not against you is for you," the point is that we are who we are either for or against the gospel of Jesus.

Just so, our relationship to *God* cannot be somehow neutral. To be for or against Jesus is to be for or against God. And we are who we are in this decision with respect to God. But so too is God who he is in relation to us. Neither is God neutral toward us, hovering per-haps in regal unconcern for the life of his lowly subjects. God's involvement in human life means that God too must decide for or against us, that God too must deter-mine his relationship to us. God offers to human beings the free gift of life in the new world of God brought near to us in Jesus. In so doing, God excludes the possi-bility of life apart from this new world. It is with this exclusion by God, this judgment of God against the old world of human sinning, that we are now concerned. Let us consider first the "what" of that divine judg-ment, and then the "why."

God determines human life to be life in relationship with himself. With this determination is excluded the possibility of life apart from this relationship. Indeed, there is no true life apart from this relationship. To be sure, there is some manner of existence, of eating and drinking, of work and sleep, of birth and death. However, in the gospel of the kingdom God determines that existence in the old world of human sinning has no meaning and purpose, and therefore has no future. The first aspect of divine judgment is therefore a resounding "No!" to the possibility of true life in the old world, the world of revolt against God.

Instead of relationship with God there is separation from God. It is no longer possible to ignore God, to resist him, to provoke and mock him, and yet still be in his presence. Not that we can ever withdraw from God entirely. Rather, God's relation to us becomes one in which he withdraws from us, sets us apart from himself. Though with us, he is against us.

Instead of personal wholeness and integrity, there is disintegration, brokenness, fragmentation. God gives the sinner over to the "weeping and gnashing of teeth," to the bitter realization of what has been lost in the forsaking of God and the torment of life apart from him.

Instead of community with others, there is exclusion and isolation, the doomed effort to build a self in solitude. The wedding feast of the Messiah is set, the guests are invited to gather around the table in fellowship and joy; those who will not come are sent away empty.

Finally, instead of the new world of God there is the world of the dead, Hades, hell. The world of the dead is the world abandoned by God at his coming to inaugurate his kingdom. It is a world without a future, or perhaps better, a world whose future is to be without direction, without movement, without life, without fulfillment. The judgment of God is that those who will not participate in the new world of the kingdom must perish with the old.

The "what" of divine judgment is, then, the condemnation of the world of human sinning. What about the "why"? Why does God judge us? The first answer is that God judges us because he is righteous. Recall that we understand this to mean that God is always God in all his ways. Even though God truly commits himself, stakes his very identity, to a relationship with his creatures, he can and will always remain who he is in this relationship. God is not mocked. He will not be put into a position in which he is forced to act other than as his identity prescribes. When human beings sin against God, they implicitly petition God to accept and sanction a relationship that is contrary to what God wills. To sin is to silently request that the divine will for human life be compromised in favor of a contrary human will. It is to ask God not to be God. Therefore, it is a direct affront to the righteousness of God.

But why does God judge us? Granted the affront to the righteousness of God—why must God react so severely? God stakes his very identity on his relationship to his creatures. His relationship with humanity is not a fulfillment of his own need; it is, rather, a gracious commitment to the good of the creature for its own sake. God therefore takes the life of the creature seriously, with far greater concern than we have for ourselves. So the severity of God's judgment is but the negative consequence of this infinite concern.

Furthermore, God's righteousness, as we have seen, means the intrinsic worthiness of God. God's relationship to his creatures is such that his own worthiness is enacted and made manifest. When the creature sins against God, the worthiness of God is called into question and finally suppressed. A lie about God is put in the place of the truth about God. God therefore judges the world of human sinning, to once again enact and manifest his own intrinsic worth, his glory. A relationship in which one partner is forced to compromise his own character is no relationship at all. The only possible recourse is for God to withdraw from that relationship—which is death to the sinner.

The second answer, and perhaps the more surprising answer, to the why of divine judgment is because of God's care for humanity. God condemns the world of human sinning because he judges life in the power of sin not worth living. God cares for human beings, and the gospel attests that life in the new world of God is the only life in which human beings can experience the fulfillment of their being. Now, here more than anywhere, it must be stressed that this is *God's* judgment, not ours. We are certainly in no position to assess the possibilities of life in revolt against God with any measure of truth. We are neither able to fully justify such a life, nor indeed able to fathom its emptiness. God's judgment is and remains his own; though we can know and trust it, we cannot comprehend it.

Trust it? How indeed is it possible to trust a God who sets himself against us when we turn from him?

Judgment and trust, judgment and love, seem to be mutually exclusive. If anything, we say, the God of judgment belongs to the Old Testament, while the gospel of the New Testament proclaims only a God of love. What is wrong with this perception? For one thing, readers of the New Testament are constantly running up against texts of judgment that render such a perception invalid. It is no wonder that Marcion, the original architect of such a view, had to edit and expurgate the New Testament so seriously to find such a view. More importantly, we cannot separate our experience of the "No!" of divine judgment from the "Yes!" of divine caring. If we do, we find it impossible to find our way from the one to the other. Both in God, and in our experience, a duality is created that tears apart the very fabric of our existence.

"Though he slay me, yet will I trust in him" (Job 13:15, KJV). What does this statement of Job mean? Is it a gluttony for punishment and self-loathing? Or is it blind obedience to a capricious and vengeful deity? No, it expresses the attitude of the gospel of the kingdom, the gospel of Jesus Christ: even God's "No!" to the life of sin is for the good of the sinner. I can never know the mercy of God until, full of humble trust, I hear him condemn my own life apart from him.

Biblical Texts for Consideration

Sin and Guilt

    Exodus 20:1–17
    Matthew 23
    Matthew 25
    John 8:34–47
    1 John 2:15–17
        (continued)

Biblical Texts for Consideration
(continued)

Affliction and Oppression

Jeremiah 22:13–17
Matthew 5:17–48
Matthew 7:1–5
Romans 8:1–11
Galatians 5:16–21
James 4:1–12

The Judgment of God

Deuteronomy 28:15–68
Matthew 18:23–35
Luke 13:34–35
Romans 1:18–32

4

GOD THE REDEEMER

THE NEW world of the kingdom of God has been announced in the gospel of Jesus Christ. The presence of God, and the power of God, have acted in him to bring that world near to human life. The old world of sin and oppression has been exposed for what it is. The revolt of humanity against the goodness and righteousness of God has made its last stand in the face of the coming of the kingdom. The judgment of God against the sin of the world has gone forth.

Where does it all come together? What results from the thrust into the world of the reality of the kingdom? What real difference does it make in human life? In this section, we shall consider the heart of the matter—the mighty work of God in redeeming us from our sin. First of all, we shall see how the judgment of God finds its resolution on the cross of Jesus Christ. In the second section, we shall explore how the blessing of the new world of God finds its resolution in the resurrection of Jesus from death. And third, we shall consider how it is that the death and resurrection of Jesus mean something for us, and not only for him. Finally, we shall consider the time of the coming of the new world of God: Is it here, or must we wait?

The Curse of God

THE GOSPEL of Jesus expresses the judgment of God against human sin, the judgment of divine righteousness as well as the judgment of divine caring. Where does the judgment finally lead? The Gospels make clear the answer to this question by their telling of the story of the crucifixion, their depiction of the death of Jesus on the cross. Their answer is that the judgment of God, with increasing tempo and weight as the passion narrative unfolds, is borne by him. Jesus Christ, the Son of God and Son of man, becomes the one who is judged. The trajectory of divine judgment regarding human sinning makes a straight line to Calvary.

As the Gospel narratives unfold, it becomes clear that the telling of Jesus' life begins to take on the life story of a sinner, a guilty sinner who is to meet his judgment. It is not that Jesus begins to sin. Rather, the Gospels make clear that though he takes on the life story of a sinner, it is a supreme act of obedience to God that drives Jesus into the circumstances of his death. Jesus is not only innocent, not only "without sin"; Jesus is obedient, seeking to fulfill the divine will to his own destruction. As the Garden of Gethsemane makes clear, and as the Gospel of John in particular confesses, Jesus "lays down his life" even as it is taken from him by the violent forces of evil. That is, he makes his own life story take on the characteristic ending of the story of a sinner.

Not only does his end come to resemble the judged death of a sinner, but it even begins to appear as *the* death of *the* sinner. As one hears the story of the cross, one hears not simply of a sinner's death. The Gospels give the impression that here at the trial of Jesus, and at his suffering and death upon the cross, the world's greatest sinner has died. Judgment day has come for this man. What happens is not simply a particularly gruesome death for a deserving man; it is the second death, the final disposition of divine wrath against one who, because of the sentence, must indeed be supremely guilty.

On the cross of Jesus the judgment of God is carried out against the sin of this man. What is this judgment? It is, first of all, the judgment of isolation. Jesus dies supremely alone. To be sure, to some extent we all die in isolation. No one can die for us, and in some sense no one can die with us, or truly be with us when we die. Yet even in death we are aware of a community of finitude that we share with others. As more or less good people, we take to our death a community of support and caring and memory. But in his death, Jesus is shunned, ostracized, mocked, betrayed. On the road to Jerusalem his closest friends begin to leave him, one by one, until only he is left to face the cross. He is cut off from family, from friends, from followers, not by his own action, but by their cowardice and betrayal. He is left to his fate by those who had professed their love. Such is the desert of the sinner: to die without the community of humanity that was forsaken by a lifetime of greed, of pride, of egotism.

The day of judgment has come upon this man, furthermore, in that his life is taken away from him. This means, first of all, that he becomes a thing in the hands of others. He is no longer master of his own fate, no longer *dominus actorum suorum*, no longer an active agent in his own life story. Instead, he is passed around from disciples to Jews to Romans; he is shamed and mocked and abused, without any recourse to action. Like a sinner going to his judgment, his life is over; there is left for him only the agony of reaping the bitter fruit of judgment.

Finally, the judgment of this man is, quite simply, his death. Jesus Christ is nailed up on the cross and dies. It is no ordinary death that he dies, but a violent and accursed death. He dies a criminal in the eyes of the Romans, and a blasphemer in the eyes of the Jews; he dies an incomprehensible and tragic mistake in the eyes of his followers, his friends, his family. This death is more than the end of a life. It is the "second death," the death of judgment, the final annihilation of the sinner whose life, in God's eyes, is not worth living. It is the death of divine anger against the folly and blasphemy of human rebellion against God. This death is hell.

What are we saying? We are saying that the death of Jesus Christ on the cross is not a "symbol" for something. It is not a symbol of sacrificial love, for example, nor is it a symbol of the redemptive power of suffering for others, or for passive resistance. In his own strange way, Feuerbach was right: we will understand the cross when we pay attention, not to the thing signified, but to the signifier; not to some mysterious truth, but to the reality. The reality of this passion narrative is the day of judgment that has come upon this man, Jesus of Nazareth, this One who proclaimed the coming of the new world of God, this One who healed our diseases, this One who opened the eyes of the blind. The event does not symbolize anything; it simply is the case that this man dies—guilty.

What does it mean for Jesus of Nazareth that he dies on the cross, judged as a sinner? His journey to the cross is the final act of a life of obedience to God. "Yet, not my will but yours be done," says Jesus in the Garden of Gethsemane (Luke 22:42). The uniqueness and mystery of this person is at least partly disclosed by this commitment to carry out the will of God despite the cost, even the cost of his own life. We must not be mistaken: it is not simply the self-sacrifice of a martyr that is involved here, but the cursed death of a sinner judged by God. The obedience of Jesus unto death bears on its shoulders not only finitude but the very evil that Jesus lived to cast out. Jesus did not want to die in this way; everything he preached taught possibilities for life and death that ran exactly counter to what he faced on Calvary. Nevertheless, he willed what God willed—for us.

His journey to the cross is likewise the final act of a life of compassion for others. He accepted the lot of others as his own lot—for their sake. As Jesus taught, if you seek to keep your own life in the face of the new world of God, you will lose it. But if you lose your own life for the sake of the gospel, you will find it. It was not simply death that he endured; it was also shameful and violent abuse and suffering at the hands of others. Though we often lose sight of it in a sea of spiritualizing about the cross, the Gospel picture of the crucifixion is painfully detailed about the abuse Jesus suffered during his trial and execution. Receiving exactly the opposite of the treatment of a king, he was mocked, degraded, humiliated. He suffered, not what he deserved, but what we deserve, what his captors and tormenters deserved. Why? He accepted for himself the deserts of others, that they might be free from the judgment that is theirs.

Furthermore, he goes to the cross a free human being. Now, his freedom certainly is not apparent on the surface of things. Indeed, quite the opposite; Jesus appears a mere thing, handed around from party to party. The texts make clear, however, that Jesus does not protest such injustice. He does not protest his innocence when treated as guilty. He does not will the life-ending of a sinner—Gethsemane makes that clear. Yet he accepts it nevertheless, and through this acceptance faces his executioners a free person. Sin and evil are the bondage of the self; Jesus alone accepts this bondage as his own, that those for whom he died might be set free.

Finally—and here we come to the heart of the matter—the death of Jesus on the cross means his abandonment, by his followers and by God. Where he proclaimed love for neighbor and relatedness between human beings, he is left to be alone by those he knew. Where Jesus proclaimed relationship with God in the new world of the kingdom, at his death Jesus is forsaken, abandoned, left alone in his estrangement by God his Father. The cross of Jesus is a death, but it is so much more than simply the cessation of a living human being. It is the second death—final, definitive, complete estrangement from God, the torment of "weeping and gnashing of teeth." That which Jesus proclaims as the judgment of the kingdom of God against all human sin he now accepts as his own final experience. "My God, my God, why have you forsaken me?" The ancient creed was right when it confessed that "he descended into hell." Here, on the cross of Jesus, judgment day has come; the gates of hell are open wide to receive a sinner in his condemnation.

Jesus suffers his fate alone on the cross, but the story of the crucifixion makes clear that we are there too. The rest of humanity is involved in this death on the cross. There are first of all the Jews, the people of God, those from whom Jesus himself came and to whom he preached the good news of the kingdom. Though some, such as Nicodemus, were able to see and to hear the voice of God and the act of God in the life of Jesus, the Bible attests that the people of God treated Jesus in a manner consistent with the history of their sin. They despised and rejected him who had come to save them. They judge him by the law that he himself fulfilled. They finally hand him over to their worst enemies to die the most degrading death between two criminals. The Jews are there at the cross of Christ to carry out violence against the truly righteous in the name of God's religion.

The Romans too are there. There is no pretense of a higher, divine authority to justify their presence. Their own might gives them the right to dispose of this human life. What is the motive for their execution of Jesus? Why did Pontius Pilate finally give in to the people of God, seemingly against his own instincts about Jesus? The Gospel story does not ascribe much of a motive to Pilate now, nor to the Roman authorities throughout the life of Jesus. That does not mean that they are thereby innocent. The Jews appeal to the religion of God, but the Romans appeal to nothing but their own power over human life. Here at the cross of Jesus is the wanton violence of worldly power in any and every form.

The disciples of Jesus are likewise involved in the crucifixion, but they are not there at the cross. They have run away because they are afraid, afraid to be with Jesus in his death. Jesus had taught them the cost of discipleship, but they were unwilling to pay it. Who cannot understand what happened here? Who does not want to save his or her life when the time comes? Is anything more important than life itself? But the story of Peter's denial makes clear that there is more involved here than simple self-preservation. Peter is unwilling even to identify with this man, much less to share his fate. The way of the cross is for Peter a matter of shame. He becomes angry even at the very suggestion that he is somehow a party to the destiny of this man Jesus of Nazareth. It is not simply fear of death that moves him, but a kind of primal shame at the lot of humankind and his own lot. The worst feeling would be the sense that one is somehow able truly to see beyond this miserable fate. No, there is nothing to be done: "I do not know the man."

Finally, humanity is there at the crucifixion in the faceless, nameless crowd that gathers on Golgotha to see what will become of him. They have followed him throughout his life, for he has provided them on occasion a truly astonishing spectacle. So they follow him to his death to see whether it too will offer something to watch.

Are they innocent? Are the nameless crowds of humanity that walk our streets, the poor and the marginalized, the people without names because they are without any significance in history and culture, are these people innocent in this death? No, they too are finally there at the cross, not only as spectators but also as executioners. They are moved by forces beyond their control to cry out for his death, even to the extent of preferring the release of a notorious political revolutionary.

The Jews, the Romans, the disciples, the crowd; all were there to deliver Jesus over to his death. None stood with him who had preached the gospel of God among them. Yet there is one exception, which all the Gospels carefully record. Citing the Gospel of Mark:

> There were also women looking on from a distance; among them were Mary Magdalene, and Mary the mother of James the younger and of Joses, and Salome. These used to follow him and provided for him when he was in Galilee; and there were many other women who had come up with him to Jerusalem.
>
> (Mark 15:40–41)

These women were not there to hand him over, or to deny him in his death. They were there to witness what took place, to see in his death what Mary Magdalene had seen in his life: the presence and power of God. By God's grace they were there, against the stream of the rest of humanity, looking on from afar to see and hear the grim judgment of God on this man Jesus.

What, finally, does the cross of Jesus mean to God? How is God involved in the crucifixion of Jesus Christ? At crucial points in the story of Jesus—his baptism and

107

his transfiguration—the Gospels attest a divine expression of pleasure in the person of Jesus: "You are my Son, the Beloved; with you I am well pleased." According to the Gospel of John (chs. 14–17), the Father loves the Son with a love that is eternal, so much so that the Bible can simply say, "God is love." God is this relationship of love between the Father and the Son in the fellowship of the Spirit, and this eternal love of God is the very love that God extends to his creatures.

Now, *this* is the God about whom we now ask: How is God involved in the crucifixion? Where is God in the suffering and death of this, his beloved Son? Where is God as Jesus is mocked and scourged by the hideous Roman police? when he is derided by the crowds of God's "children"? when he is betrayed by his disciples and left alone to die? The Gospels make their testimony to this great truth of the Christian gospel by their silence. By "the definite plan and foreknowledge of God," this Jesus of Nazareth has been delivered to be crucified and killed. God has offered him as a sacrifice for sins, offered up by the hands of sinful Israel. God has indeed abandoned Jesus as the fitting end to the life story of a sinner. God is not there at the cross because God has judged this man Jesus to be guilty. Just as Jesus was baptized by John "to fulfill all righteousness," so he is now judged and condemned by God in order to fulfill all unrighteousness. He carries sin and evil to their dreadful conclusion, "for God so loved the world that he gave his only Son." Christ loved me and gave himself for me.

The Blessing of God

JESUS CHRIST is dead on the cross. He is taken down by some interested parties and placed in a nearby tomb. His body is prepared for burial, and the tomb is sealed. The judgment of God against this sinner has taken its toll. He has borne out to its bitter end the guilt and condemnation of human revolt against God. He is without any further possibilities for life, or such life as can be had apart from God. God has judged his life no longer worth living, and taken it from him. He has not simply ceased living; he has died the final death of human life under the divine curse. "It is finished."

What now of the gospel of the new world of the kingdom of God? What now of righteousness, peace, and justice, of relationship with God? The power of sin and evil has overtaken this man who once preached a world with God rather than against God. Now the judgment of God has rightly closed out the account of life apart from God. The Romans are unconcerned, being used to the power of the sword. The Jews are suspicious; some are aware that something more is at stake here than another incipient heresy. The disciples are scattered and purposeless. Even the women who witnessed his death can only grieve at the death of this, their hope. All is ended with this life-ending.

But on the third day of his burial something happens that changes everything. First the women, and then the rest of the disciples, become aware of the fantastic and unheard-of news: Jesus is alive! He is risen from the dead! He lives! It is not a ghost, not a spirit of Jesus which has somehow escaped the tomb of the body. It is he, the person, the man Jesus of Nazareth!

The resurrection of Jesus from the dead is the culmination of the blessing of God just as surely as the cross is the ending of the curse of God. Yet the resurrection is not the companion piece of a "matched set" with the cross. It does not somehow complete the event of the crucifixion, as if Jesus' death on the cross were a mere prelude to the main event of the resurrection. God acted once to judge human sin on the cross of Christ; and, thanks be to God, God acted yet again to raise him to new life beyond the grave. We can and must bear witness to both acts of God, but they are two acts, not beginning and end of the same act. For, in and of itself, Jesus' death is real and complete, final and definitive. New life beyond death is just that: a new life whose possibility is not contained in the old.

In his resurrection from the dead, Jesus Christ is vindicated by God as Lord of the world. He who lives eternally "in the form of God" had condescended to become like unto us, even unto death on the cross, in order to redeem us from our sins. The glory and mystery of the gospel is this great act of God's self-giving love. The resurrection of Jesus Christ from the dead vindicates, declares, and manifests this mystery to the eyes of faith. In his resurrection, Jesus Christ is revealed as the Lord of the world, the reconciler of humanity, the one purpose of God in creation and redemption. The Christian faith is resurrection faith; it is faith in the living Lord Jesus Christ, who died as savior of the world.

The Gospels present their readers with a detailed picture of the *terminus a quo* of the resurrection, and with a portrait of the *terminus ad quem;* but they hardly mention the transition between the two, the movement from the death of Christ to the living Christ. Let us consider each of these in turn. The *terminus a quo* of the resurrection is the crucified Jesus, dead and buried. The Gospels leave no doubt that he is really and truly dead with the kind of finality that only comes from the judgment of God. The Apostles' Creed makes this point where it says that Jesus "descended into hell," where only the condemned sinner belongs. This means that the resurrection can in no sense be a matter of preserving some part of the self for life after death. In Western culture, both ancient and modern, it has often been held that human persons possess a faculty that, because of its likeness to the eternity of "reason" or "idea" or "God," points beyond the death of the body. This doctrine of the immortality of the soul is dramatically opposite to the biblical witness concerning the resurrection, as centrally determined by the resurrection of Jesus. The whole person, no matter how one describes the various faculties, or parts, or dimensions, perishes in death, and in the condemnation of the sinner.

So it is also with the *terminus ad quem* of the resurrection. It is not a "spirit" or "soul" of Jesus that somehow escapes the tomb of the body and lives eternally. It is, rather, the whole person of Jesus, who once was dead but now is alive. He can be recognized by his former companions; he moves about from place to place; he eats and drinks; he speaks with his followers.

He is the same and yet not the same. While he moves about from place to place, he suddenly appears in the midst of his followers. Though recognizable as Jesus of Nazareth, he can be mistakenly identified by even his closest companions. Though he eats to confirm his corporeality, he no longer goes about with the disciples as he used to, no longer shares the routine of daily life—eating and drinking, labor and rest, fellowship and privacy. Somehow he is apart from them in a way that he never was when he was with them before his death. Paul speaks of this mode of life as the possession of a "spiritual body," an imperishable and incorruptible form of existence that comes only from the grace and mercy of God.

Who is he? Who is the resurrected Jesus? He is the One whose life and death on the cross have been vindicated by God. Though he dies the death of a sinner under the hand of the divine judgment, unacceptable to the righteousness of God, God turns to this man in complete acceptance and says yes to his life. God accepts the unacceptable. More than that, he sets this man on a new course that is far better than the old. He does not simply restore Jesus to his former life; he gives him new life that, while it nourishes and sustains the same identity as the old, can provide a matrix for existence that far exceeds the possibilities of the old. What is this new life? Though the Gospels do not name it directly, it is clearly nothing but the new world of the kingdom of God. The resurrected Jesus is the first citizen in the new world of God. Or, to use the words of John's Gospel, he is the first to possess "eternal life." It is still the same Jesus, but it is a new world in which he lives, a world in which sin and evil have been crushed and defeated, in which the power of the evil one has been cut out, where disease and brokenness are replaced by wholeness, and where death itself is dead.

What of the transition from this *terminus a quo* to this *terminus ad quem?* What do the Gospels say about the resurrection itself? What of this turning point from death to life for Jesus of Nazareth? First of all, the Gospels, together with the rest of the New Testament witness, are agreed that it is an act of God. That is, the resurrection does not just "happen" as other things happen; it is a startling, amazing, unheard-of event wrought by God. Indeed, so directly is it the act of God that close analysis of the event is not possible—no more possible than close analysis of God himself. The limits of the knowledge of the event of the resurrection are the same as the limits of our knowledge of God: that which one truly knows is that which God graciously makes known. On the one hand, this means that attempts to "prove" the resurrection as a historical event can only prove something other than the resurrection. Such attempts can only "prove" what is within the rational grasp of the human mind, and therefore only a false image of the living Jesus.

On the other hand, we must not allow the inherent mystery of the event to devolve into amorphous obscurity. The resurrection is not a symbol of some deep, hidden human experience—not a symbol, for example, of the Easter faith of the disciples. While hidden in the mystery of God, it is nonetheless real. Indeed, as an event of God, it is more real than anything that simply "happens" and that is therefore within the rational grasp of the human mind. Though he was dead, yet now he lives. How? We cannot say; but we do not thereby abandon the reality of our confession of the resurrection.

The resurrection is the definitive and complete fulfillment of the promise of divine blessing in human life.

It accomplishes for this man, Jesus of Nazareth, what God wills for every human being, and has willed from the foundation of the world. It establishes a life beyond death, that is, a life free from mortality and the threat of final estrangement from God resulting from human sin. The raised and living Jesus of Nazareth is a human being who will not die. Through the grace of divine blessing, his life is eternal.

Furthermore, it is a life beyond death free from the power of sin. Through his death on the cross, Jesus came to be identified with human sin. He was handed over to the power of sin, delivered up to the disposing of sinful humanity. In the Romans, the Jews, the disciples, the sin of the world was there at his death to overtake and vanquish him. But the risen Christ is no more in the power of sin, no more delivered up to its bondage. Sin has been defeated. The living Jesus Christ is empowered by the Spirit of God, free from the reach of a defeated enemy.

Finally, it is a life freed from divine judgment. He who had been nailed to the cross a guilty sinner is, in the resurrection from the dead, proclaimed by God "not guilty." The risen Christ lives in a world of complete divine acceptance. The cup of suffering has been drunk; there is no longer a journey toward Jerusalem and the cross.

The resurrection is a life beyond death, beyond sin, beyond judgment; the threats to human fulfillment have been removed. But what is the life of the risen Lord, Jesus Christ? He appears to the disciples and declares to them that all authority has been given to him in heaven and on earth. He ascends into heaven and rules the world. He sends his Spirit to bear witness to himself in Word and sacrament. In a word, Christian faith is faith in the living Lord, Jesus Christ.

Jesus Christ has fulfilled the coming of the kingdom of God. Indeed, Jesus is now the King of kings and Lord of lords. Sin is vanquished, death itself is dead, the forces of evil are overthrown. But the resurrection of Christ calls forth resurrection *faith*. This means first of all that his rule over the world, while real and indeed public, is seen only by the eyes of faith. It is concealed from the world in the humility of the gospel itself. But more, it means that even the eyes of faith, bound to the risen Lord Jesus Christ through the power of the Spirit in the gospel, await his final appearing. Then we shall see him as he is.

The Blessed Exchange

WHAT DO the cross and resurrection of Jesus Christ mean for us? Certainly the heart of the gospel is the proclamation that in Jesus Christ we find salvation. We now turn directly to this question: What is this salvation, and how does it affect our lives?

"For our sake he made him to be sin who knew no sin, so that in him we might become the righteousness of God" (2 Cor. 5:21). The gospel proclaims that the death and resurrection of Jesus of Nazareth are not simply events in themselves, not simply isolated occurrences transpiring in the general flow of time, but events that reach out beyond themselves to include every other event and every other person. They occurred "for our sake." The death and resurrection of Jesus Christ are certainly events in the personal life story of this man, Jesus of Nazareth, who is the Son of God. We have already been able to depict in some detail the meaning these have in the gospel telling of his life story. Even now as we speak of the meaning of these events for us, we must not allow this reality to be swallowed up in a sea of self-concern and self-analysis. Indeed, as we consider this meaning according to the biblical witness, we are not at all turning from concern for Jesus to concern for self, so much as we are simply hearing and seeing what the Gospels want to say and depict about the meaning and truth of Jesus Christ for us, the love of Christ for me. Unlike other events, these events, and this life story, lay a claim on the reader, indeed announce to the reader the very meaning of his or her existence. How does this occur?

Jesus Christ reconciles us to God. That is the fundamental meaning of redemption. By his life, death, and resurrection from the dead, Jesus Christ puts us into right relation with God. Where we are exposed as sinners in radical alienation from God, God in his mercy declares us acquitted of the guilt of sin through the sacrifice of his Son. Not by our moral efforts; not by our spiritual experience; not by our deeds of justice and mercy; not by the projects and causes that we embrace and enjoin upon others; but solely by the free and sovereign grace of God in Jesus Christ are we justified—put right with God—in the cross and resurrection. It is a freely given grace which we can receive in faith, and, as we shall see, faith itself in receiving it is not a human work, but a gift of the Spirit. From beginning to end,

God saves the world in grace and mercy. This is the amazing good news of the gospel.

"For our sake," he died and rose again to help us, who could not help ourselves, and indeed who could not choose to be helped. Being redeemed by Jesus Christ is not a choice we make, for we are in no position to choose anything at all. We are in bondage to powers of sin and evil that have stolen away our freedom to choose the fulfillment of our lives. Humanity was certainly not there at the cross of Jesus to choose him as our redeemer. Jews, Romans, disciples tried to get from him what they wanted during his life, and in the end delivered him up to death because of his failure to meet their expectation of him. Jesus Christ is there for us not because we ask his help, but despite the fact that we reject his help with the primitive violence and irrational condemnation of unfettered sin and evil.

If we do not choose him to be our redeemer, how can he be there to help us, "for our sake"? In an act of inconceivable intimacy with his creatures, God was there in Christ to act for us. Unable as we were to lift ourselves out of the slough of sin, God rescued us by acting for us, or, perhaps we can say, by taking our place. The gospel of the kingdom is about a covenant relationship between God and his creatures. The cross and resurrection of Jesus Christ are the perfect fulfillment of that relationship, because in them God joins with us in our finite and sinful condition. In other words, God brings the relationship to fulfillment by taking our side in the relationship.

In Jesus Christ, God brings to fulfillment the promise of a new world of God by taking our condition upon himself, in order that he might give to us his condition. Luther called this movement of divine redemption the "blessed exchange." Jesus Christ became what we are in order that we might become what he is.

In the suffering and death of the cross, Jesus became what we are. For our sake, he took our condition upon himself; God "made him to be sin who knew no sin." As we have seen, the ending to the story of Jesus becomes the life-ending of a sinner. But it is not simply the life-ending of a sinner; as the Gospels tell it, it is the life-ending of *the* sinner, of One whom all the world joins in offering up to death, and on whom God manifests for all to see the terrible signs of the last judgment. What happens here is the death of One who faces not only his own death, but death itself; who suffers not only the judgment of his sin, but the final judgment of God against all sin; who not only becomes entangled in the circumstances of sin and evil, but on whom is poured the full fury of the gates of hell. He is thrust into this position because of his will to be where we are, to embrace us in our true condition.

In return, he freely gives us his own condition. In the resurrection of Jesus Christ from the dead, God brings to humanity new life in relationship with God. In fact, God brings to humanity nothing less than the blessed life of his only Son, Jesus Christ. Just as he had acted for us in his death on the cross, so now does he bring us along with him to new life beyond the threat of sin, of death, and of the power of evil. He can do this, and do it with effect, because he has already carried to its terrible conclusion the old life of sin and evil. Because he became what we are, so now do we become what he is.

Let us say it differently. Jesus Christ himself is God's mighty act of salvation for the world. His person and work—and not any christological or soteriological concepts—are the center of the gospel. *He* is the new world of God; *he* is our righteousness before God; *he* is our peace with God; *he* is our reconciliation with God. And that is why all righteousness of works is radically excluded—all moral transformation, all spiritual experience, all piety, all working for justice and peace, all cooperation with God of any kind—as the basis and reality of our salvation. Jesus Christ himself is God's radically free and gracious gift of salvation for the world. To speak, as Luther does, of "alien righteousness" is simply to point to him; to call for faith alone apart from all works of the law is, again, simply to point to him. By grace alone, through faith alone, because in Christ alone.

This is the redemption of God—the heart of the gospel. We can now examine it more closely. That Jesus Christ took our condition on himself and saw it through to the bitter end on the cross means for us the forgiveness of sins. He became guilty, that God might declare us "Not guilty!" Forgiveness of sins does not mean that God has for some reason come to accept our weakness. In forgiving us, God does not accept our sin. Rather, God has taken the guilt and burden and power of sin off our shoulders, and in Jesus Christ has taken it on himself. Forgiveness of sins does not mean a mitigation of the divine judgment of human sin. Rather, God has taken our judgment from us and in Jesus Christ has taken it on himself. God neither accepts human sinning nor does he wave off judgment of it. To do so would mean abandoning an evil world to its own fate. In a moment of supreme involvement with the world, God in his love for the world abandons instead his Son, Jesus Christ, that he might be with us.

The forgiveness of sins is not the divine acceptance of sin, but it is the divine mercy toward the sinner. As one who has dwelt with us, he knows our nature; as one who has withstood the violent assault of the world of sinners against himself in the days leading up to the cross, he knows the hold of the power of sin over human lives. The mercy of God's forgiveness means that God does not simply settle our accounts from a distance. Even though we are rebels against him, God deals with us by becoming intimately involved in our lives. It is not a negligent love that moves God, but a deeply caring love. Despite our sin, he wants to be in union with us, our companion, our friend. That is God's mercy to us.

The forgiveness of sins means that the life of sin is closed out as a possibility for human life. That is, God not only ceases to hold our sins to account, God takes away the power of sin in human life. To put it more decisively, in the cross of Jesus Christ we die as rebels against God. Christian doctrine has far too often been fixated on the idea of punishment, as if the cross means nothing but a kind of divine disciplinary act. The cross is *judgment*, not punishment, and judgment means a final verdict, a divine disposing of human sinners once for all. In the death of Jesus Christ on the cross the final judgment has come on all human sinning. Sin is finished! Rebellion against God is no longer possible! Death itself is dead! The forgiveness of sins means that I am no longer who I was as a sinner against God. In the death of Jesus Christ on the cross, that life is over. God neither accepts my sin, nor does he permit it; in Jesus Christ, God puts my sin to an end. The judgment of God is nothing other than the almighty grace of his redeeming love.

Jesus became what we are in order to remove the power and guilt of sin. But the redemption of God does not end there. In Jesus Christ, God gives us something else in return: righteousness. There is a righteousness that belongs to God, as we have seen; by God's righteousness we mean his determination to be who he is in all circumstances and relationships. There is also a righteousness that belongs to God's creature. The righteousness of the creature is a life that is in right relationship to God. It is not primarily moral, though it certainly involves moral behavior. Indeed, it is not about us, per se, at all; the righteousness of the creature is about our new life with God in the new world of the kingdom.

In his life, death, and resurrection from the dead, Jesus Christ is truly righteous, the complete and definitive enactment of the will of God in human life. He is himself the kingdom of God, the true and proper relation between God and humanity. And his righteousness is made perfect in his obedience unto death, even death on the cross. By his resurrection from the dead his righteousness is freely given to us. In his resurrection from death, the new world of God has come.

Through the risen Christ we are not only freed from the guilt and burden of sin, we are likewise freely given by God full participation in the blessing of the new world. In the risen Christ, we are what God wills us to be: his children in the new world. "While we still were sinners," Christ died on the cross to deliver us from our sins and was raised from the dead to give us new life with God. The righteousness of Christ is our entrance into the new world of God.

Instead of a life of judgment and condemnation, it is a new life of full divine acceptance. We are reconciled to God; we are the children of God. The struggle is over to find a God who will say yes to our lives. The God who says yes in the gospel of the risen Christ does not do so from a distance, but says yes in the most intimate relationship to who we are. As Jesus did, we cry out to God: "Abba, Father." Our righteousness in the risen Christ is not a shield that keeps us from exposure to God; it is, rather, an invitation to true closeness with God. Beyond fear, we love him.

Instead of a life under the curse of death, in the righteousness of the risen Christ we have life in abundance, eternal life. We remain finite, to be sure; that is, we are still sinful creatures and therefore come into being and pass away. But our passing is no longer surrounded by the menace of the second death, the final judgment of God against us as sinners. We shall die—to be raised with Christ to new life!

Indeed, we have died as creatures in the old world of sin and evil that has breathed its last on the cross of Christ. We are raised in a new world that has dawned in the resurrection of Jesus from the dead. Who are we in this new world? What kind of life do we have? As with the risen Christ, we are ourselves, and yet not ourselves. It is I who am raised from death in the power of God; but who I am is determined no longer by the power of sin, but by the new world of the kingdom. I am therefore transformed, the citizen of a new world. I inhabit a world in which all resistance to relationship with God has been finally overcome.

The righteousness we have in the risen Christ brings also the definitive restructuring of relationships between human beings. Just as Jesus was free to be truly present with his disciples, so are we truly present with one another. "Heaven" in the Bible is not an individual destiny beyond the grave. It is a new world in which we share our citizenship with all who call on the name of the risen Jesus. It is not less corporate, less social than our world, but more so. We share completely in the lives of others because in the life of the risen Christ we are freely given a new humanity far beyond the oppressive and treacherous forms of relationship in the old world. We learn truly to love, as we have never loved before.

One final word remains to be added to our reflections concerning the meaning of divine redemption in Jesus Christ. That is the word *grace*. God can and does redeem our lives; he turns them around, putting away the power of sin that oppresses us and setting us on a path of life that leads into the blessing of the kingdom. He does these things at infinite cost to himself. Why? What draws God into involvement with his creatures that is so costly? It is certainly not our accomplishment as God's creatures. From the beginning of human history to the very present moment, human beings have done very badly what God has given them to do. Neither is it some potentiality in us that moves God to draw us toward himself. Only a fool would assess our possibilities so brightly. God redeems us for no reason at all, other than his love for us. It is not a love that finds anything in the beloved, but a love—and only God's love is like this—that comes from the freedom of his amazing grace.

It is here in fact that the Christian gospel and modernity are most in conflict. Modernity has meant a tremendous burst of human energy in many areas of culture, from the industrial revolution, to the democratization of politics, to momentous advances in transportation and communication, and on and on. Who cannot marvel at what the last few centuries, and indeed the last few decades, have brought to the progress of civilization? But the redemption of humanity is not the omega point on this trajectory of human culture. The gospel of grace proclaims to us that God redeems because we cannot redeem ourselves; that indeed God is there to save us because we cannot but corrupt ourselves. In the light of the gospel, who cannot see that for every advance in civilization has come a corresponding degradation of human life? We have technology—and the environmental crisis; we have nuclear power—and the threat of global destruction; we have the computer—and the dehumanization of the workplace.

Perhaps we cast our nets too broadly. Perhaps it is better to speak of a human life than to speak of human culture generally. The grace of redemption means that I too am held up by the hand of God reaching down, I who am too weak and foolish to stand on my own. Opportunities for self-improvement seem to appear at every turn, but try as I might, I cannot seem to escape the myriad other opportunities for self-destruction. I cannot redeem myself, cannot bring my life to fulfillment of even the limited potential I can see for myself. Moreover, I do not reach the cross and resurrection through such reflection; rather, I can only truly see myself in this way in the light of the cross and resurrection of Jesus. Only when God redeems me do I understand that I cannot redeem myself. Only when, through some inconceivable power and overwhelming kindness from above, I find myself somehow along a way of fulfillment, do I realize just how far from it I can be, how chaotic and merciless my life is as I put it together.

On the cross of Christ, God joins us where we are, in order that through the resurrection of Jesus from the dead, God might bring us where he is. In doing so, God makes right what we have done so badly. We did not ask for God's help; indeed, if it were up to us, we would certainly refuse it. But thanks be to God, it is not up to us. Thanks be to God, he has taken our affairs into his own hands, making our destiny his intimate concern. God is with us; we are not alone. Truly, thanks be to God.

Between the Times

IN JESUS Christ, God is our redeemer; but are we redeemed? We may look around us and see little of the promised new world of the kingdom of God. Do we really see in ourselves the features of the redeemed human beings won by Christ on the cross? Indeed, what little good we might see in the world and in ourselves becomes even less noteworthy in light of the proclamation of the gospel of redemption.

According to the witness of the New Testament, redemption is already accomplished, but it is not yet complete. Or, to put it in the narrative form of the biblical witness, Jesus Christ has come once, and will come again. The disciples of Jesus live "between the times" of his first and second coming. Here we must consider what this means for our reflections on the gospel of redemption.

In Jesus Christ, God has already redeemed the world, already reconciled the world to himself in loving relationship. This is the first word of the gospel. The redemption of God is not a question mark, nor an open set, nor an incomplete process. With the finality of death on Calvary, the gospel proclaims: "It is finished." We can use a biblical concept to make this clear by speaking of the death and resurrection of Jesus as "once for all" (Rom. 6:10). "Once for all" means, first of all, that what Jesus did cannot, and need not, be done again. It cannot be done again because he alone was able and willing to do it. As the "only-begotten Son" of the Father, the unique presence of God in this human life, Jesus of Nazareth acts for our sake in a way that no other human being can act. He loves others with a compassion that comes from his closeness to the divine love. His journey to Jerusalem and the cross are the acts of One who obeys God fully from the heart, even to his own hurt.

What Jesus did for us on the cross need not be done again—because it is already done! Jesus so fully represents us before God that what happens to him, happens to us. Our sin is forgiven, because he is judged a sinner. Our blessing is lavished on us, because he is raised from the dead. Our life story, from birth to death to beyond death, is taken up into his life story by the grace of God. His life story cannot and need not be repeated by ours, even symbolically, in order to be meaningful and true. It can be followed by us only because it is already meaningful and true "once for all."

"Once for all" means furthermore that there is nothing left over of human destiny that is not decisively settled in the death and resurrection of Jesus. We are who we are as determined by the divine willing of our relationship with himself and our self-willed bondage to the power of sin and revolt against God. Nothing is true about us beyond this twofold determination. No possible threat to our fulfillment remotely compares to the power of sin, and this threat is once for all removed from us by the cross. No greater fulfillment awaits us than friendship with God in the new world, and this is once for all accomplished in the resurrection. There are surely many smaller truths about our lives and relationships, important truths that make us who we are as individual human beings different from others; these smaller but important truths are not suppressed by the once for all of redemption. But the gospel proclaims that none of these smaller truths—the height and weight of my body, my talents and goals, my family and friends, my time and place—compete with the twofold determination of my life as disclosed in the gospel. Therefore, we can say of his story: *De te fabula narratur.*

Even so, what of the not yet? Why is the redemption of God not yet evident in the world around us and in our own lives? We can begin our answer with the biblical witness to the appearing of Jesus at the end of time.

All is accomplished in the cross and resurrection of Christ, but not all is made manifest. The redemption of God is real and unimaginably effective; but it is concealed "in Christ" and not yet revealed for every eye to see and ear to hear. The appearing of Christ at the end of time will therefore mean first of all a definitive revelation of the reality of redemption accomplished at Calvary. We can certainly know the redemption now by faith in him, the one in whom it is now concealed. What is now true by faith in him will one day be true also in the sight of all.

Moreover, the final appearing of Jesus will bring with it universal revelation. We do not now know how many, or who, believe in the gospel of redemption. We do not know the mystery of God's will to save the world. The biblical witness is that in the final appearing of the Savior all the world will see and hear and know the salvation of God. Now he is concealed from the world in the swaddling clothes of the manger and the humility of the Christian witness, but then he shall appear to everyone as the victor over sin and savior of the world.

Finally, when he comes what is now true *for* us will be true *in* us. He lived and died and rose again for our sake; as we have seen, this means that the truth about our lives is really and effectively determined by this, God's act to redeem us. Because it is his act, it is more true, more real, than our own resistance to it. Nevertheless, according to the gospel, what Jesus Christ has done for us has not yet been done once for all in us. We are freed from sin by him, but we are not yet free from sin in ourselves; we are freed by him from guilt before God, but we are not yet free from the disobedience that so angers God; we are freed by him from the power of evil in human life, but we are not free in ourselves from the bondage of the will. We are freed by him from the sting of death, and yet we still die—to be raised by him. Now, there is clearly an order here in the biblical witness of super- and subordinate. It is infinitely more true what we are "in him" than what we are "in ourselves." Nevertheless, the will of God is that we become in ourselves what we already are in him. This takes place in two ways: On the one hand, it takes place in the simple act of faith and the life of discipleship. That is, it takes place in the Christian life; we shall have occasion to consider this more fully in the next chapter. It takes place, on the other hand, when Jesus Christ will come again. At his coming, what is already true *about* us in him will be true *in* us. It will truly be the end of the age, the end of time itself—that is, the present time of human revolt against God, which is the time we know now. It will be what the Bible calls heaven: a new world of God where there is no sin, and where blessing abounds.

There is an "already" and a "not yet" to salvation; is there an already and a not yet of judgment? On the one hand, the judgment of us all has been taken upon his shoulders, and yet we will one day face the Judge. Who is the Judge whom we are to face? He is the very One who has taken our judgment upon himself. The judgment of humanity is upon him; and yet all humanity, those who believe and those who do not believe, will one day face the Judge.

What of the time between the times, the time between the first and second appearing of Jesus Christ?

What of our time? Is Jesus only *for* us, and in no sense *in* us? While the Bible makes clear that for the definitive revelation of redemption we must await the return of Jesus in hope, it also makes clear that we do not wait alone, or in vain. First of all, we see Jesus, who is himself the first citizen of the new world of God. He is the firstfruits of the kingdom of God, and as such is a divine sign of that which is to come. The "not yet" of the redemption of God does not precede the "already" but follows it. That is, because he has already come, therefore the kingdom has not yet been finally revealed. And because he has already come, the not yet is a formed hope, not an amorphous wish for better times.

Moreover, Jesus has not left us alone to await his coming. He has left us with the "seal of the Spirit," the presence of God in our hearts and lives, which directs us away from the world of sin and evil and toward the coming kingdom of God. It is not a different spirit than the presence of God in Jesus himself; that is, when we turn to the Spirit we are not turning away from the Christ who died and rose again for our sake. Rather, just as God sent Jesus into the world to redeem us, so Jesus, together with the Father, sent the Spirit to be in us while we wait between the times. On the cross, he acted for us; in the Spirit, he is with us; and we wait for that day when Christ the Lord will be all in all.

The seal of the Spirit gives meaning and purpose to the time between the times. It is a time for us to act with God in service of the kingdom. Even in a world filled with sin and evil, God wills to rescue from bondage those who live in the Spirit. Indeed, it is an opportunity for the followers of Jesus to share in the task of proclaiming the new world of God as he proclaimed it. We exist in this time to bear witness to Jesus Christ and to live in the power of the Spirit of freedom. Through bearing witness in word and life, we become what in Christ we already are: forgiven sinners who act in relationship with God in the service of the new world.

When will he come again? How long must we wait until Jesus Christ will come to reveal definitively what he has accomplished for our sake on the cross? The Bible has one simple answer to this question: He will come soon. Let us consider this answer more fully. The chorus of biblical witnesses concerning this issue makes clear that the testimony that he will come soon is *not* a prediction. It is not a forecast of when it will happen, and that for two reasons. First of all, according to the word of Jesus, no one knows the time of his coming— not even Jesus himself. His coming is a decision of God for which we must wait; the capacity to predict it would mean the arrogation to oneself of the power of divine knowledge. Second, one cannot predict the coming of Jesus because it is not a future moment in our time. Instead, it is new time, a new age, a new world. A prediction can have meaning only within a unitary time frame. The coming of Jesus will not be an event in our future, as much as the end of our time—past, present, and future—and the definitive manifestation of that new time which drew near to us in the life, death, and resurrection of Jesus.

If it is not a prediction, what does it mean to say that he will come soon? It means first of all that our time, the past, present, and future of the old world of sin and rebellion against God, has already been circumscribed by that new time of the kingdom of God. Our past is judged and forgiven on the cross of Jesus; our present is the eternal now of his presence with us and in us; our future is the horizon of his coming in glory to complete his redemption. "Soon," then, does not answer the question of when he will come in reference to our time. Rather, it redirects our attention away from our time to the new time of the kingdom of God. Now, that is not to say that the coming of Christ is timeless, as if the present time is swallowed up in transcendent atemporality. No, he *will* come; our time *will* end; the kingdom *will* be revealed and established. But the "future" of this future tense is not our future, it is his future, his time, and his new age. To say it another way, the "soon" of the biblical witness does not predict the quantity of time before his coming, but stipulates the quality or nature of our present age—it is not to remain, but to give way to his kingdom.

Second, to say that he will come soon expresses an attitude of urgent watchfulness on the part of those who believe in Christ. To believe in Christ means to expect his return at any moment; it means to have every moment transformed by the hope of his coming. As we shall consider more fully in the next chapter, it means to live my life knowing that the time I have been given, and indeed the time of the world in which I live, is radically conditioned by the coming kingdom of God. If I do not live for the new world of Jesus Christ, I waste my time. Because I cannot predict when he will come, I must expect him every moment. This gives to every moment of my life a quality of sobriety, but also a quality of quiet comfort and joy that transcends my capacity to manage my time.

Between the times, we await his time. How long, O Lord?

Biblical Texts for Consideration

The Curse of God

Psalm 22
Matthew 26–27
Mark 14–15
Luke 22–23
John 18–19

The Blessing of God

Matthew 28
Mark 16
Luke 24
John 20–21

The Blessed Exchange

Isaiah 53
Romans 4:25
Romans 5
1 Corinthians 15
2 Corinthians 5:16–21
Galatians 3:10–14
Ephesians 2
Colossians 2:8–15; 3:1–4

Between the Times

Psalm 130
Romans 8:18–25
1 Thessalonians 4:13–5:11
Hebrews 9–10
2 Peter 3:1–13

5

THE CHRISTIAN LIFE

THE GOSPEL is not only a truth about our lives, it seeks to be a truth in our lives. Through Jesus Christ, God wills, according to the gospel, to touch in the most intimate way the people we are. God wills indeed to make us new people, people who are fit for citizenship in the new world of the kingdom, people in whom the relationship of the covenant fulfilled in Christ will come to fruition. The life, death, and resurrection of Jesus are for our sake, but they are not elements of a divine drama to which we are merely spectators. They are rather truths about our lives so deep and significant that those who embrace them become different people, new people. They become Christians.

How does this happen? What occurs so that, here on the one hand is the story of redemption in Jesus, and here on the other hand is my story as redeemed by Jesus? There are two answers in the Bible, but they are really not two but one. I become a Christian, first of all, through hearing the word of the gospel in faith. The good news of redemption is told to me, and I believe.

The second answer of the Bible is that the reality of the new life in Christ is sealed in my heart by the Spirit of God. The Spirit of God comes into us; through the Spirit of God, the risen Christ is not "out there" but "in here," in my heart; "it is no longer I who live, but . . . Christ who lives in me."

Baptism is the physical sign that corresponds to the death of the old life and incorporation into the radically new life that is given me by the Spirit. The Lord's Supper is the physical sign that, whenever I partake of it, confirms before my very eyes the real relationship I have to the crucified and risen Lord.

But who is the Spirit of God? The Bible does not answer this question in the same way that it answers the question of the identity of Jesus and the identity of the Father of Jesus. There is not a gospel of the Spirit, a story of the Spirit, a description of the Spirit. The Spirit is there with Jesus at his birth and comes upon him in his baptism; however, the gospel is not about the Spirit but about Jesus. The Spirit descends on the early disciples at Pentecost with power and signs of wonder, bringing the new world of God into human life. However, the coming of the Spirit on the early disciples does not transform the book of Acts into an abstract story of the Spirit but ties the Spirit directly to the spread of the gospel, the word of God.

The Spirit of God is the power of the new world of God in Christ poured into our hearts.[1] The Spirit is God himself making the redemption of Jesus unimaginably effective in the lives of human beings. The Spirit opens our eyes, lifts up our hearts, frees us for the new life. Yet even as we say this, we must remember that the

Spirit is the power of the *gospel,* not our power. Through the power of the Spirit we come to belong to Jesus. Through the power of the Spirit, we come to have faith, love, and hope.

When we become Christians, we become what we already are. The logic is strange, but according to the Bible absolutely irreversible. Becoming a Christian is not a process that leads forward to a state-of-being at the end of the process; it is rather a process that brings into our lives the identity that is already ours through the grace of God. Becoming a Christian does not create our identity—it accepts it. It makes real what is already true. Who we are has once for all been determined by God in the sacrifice of his Son. But we have not yet become who we are.

We can say it differently by saying that faith is a necessary response to what God has done for me in Jesus Christ. In the life, death, and resurrection of Jesus Christ, God has acted to save the world. When I hear this good news of the gospel, my life is claimed by God. I am brought face-to-face with the power of God unto salvation. Faith means receiving the free gift of salvation that God has offered to me in Jesus Christ. Faith is the act of saying yes to God's yes to me in the gospel of Christ.

Becoming a Christian is the act of receiving the life that Jesus has redeemed for us. One word summarizes this life: freedom. Where once we were in bondage to the power of guilt and sin, now we are free. Becoming a Christian means to receive this freedom given to us by Christ in the power of the Spirit. Not to do so is simply to remain unfree, to remain in bondage to the powers of the old world, which is passing away. But freely to will the redemption that is ours in Jesus Christ is to bring to fulfillment the relationship with God that God desires. It is a decision to God's glory and our blessing together. Becoming a Christian means freely to believe, freely to love, and freely to hope.

Faith

BECOMING A Christian means being put right with God, and so becoming a new creation, a new person. It certainly does not mean becoming something other than human; indeed, to become a Christian means precisely to become fully human, if by that one means to become what God made us to be. Yet becoming a Christian does not mean an enhancement of our experienced humanity, perhaps through some feeling of transcendence, or inner transformation, or behavioral modification. One cannot find one's way to God in Christ through exploration of the potentialities of the human self. The Christian witness is that God finds his way to us through creation of a new self.

Becoming a Christian means entering a personal relationship with God, through Jesus Christ, in the power of the Spirit. The new person of which we speak is nothing other than the self in this relationship to God. Where once one could measure one's self in isolation, estimating as high or low the various possibilities and realities of human personality and experience, now one can do so no longer. The human self is what it is through its relationship to God. As we have seen, it does not even "choose" this relationship, if by that one means the acting out of various alternatives presented to the self. The relationship to God is fulfilled from above, by God; and it comes to us as fulfillment, as reality, not as possibility or potentiality. God presents us with the fulfillment of relationship with himself, accomplished on the cross, rescuing us from bondage to sin and giving us a new direction in life. Becoming a Christian means freely accepting this relationship, and freely walking in this new direction.

We enter this new relationship with God when we have faith in Jesus Christ. Let us consider the Christian concept of faith more closely. To have faith means, first of all, to recognize the truth of the gospel as the truth of one's own life. There on the cross of Calvary hangs a man who not only dies his own death, but also dies my death; there in the empty tomb of Easter is the resurrection to life not only of this man, but of me. There in this man, Jesus of Nazareth, is enacted a relationship with God that is my relationship, my rescue from the ravages of sin and evil, the redemption of my life. Who am I? What is the point of my life? Faith means, first of all, the recognition that the answer to these questions is nailed to the cross on Calvary. I am the one whom God sought out at the expense of his only-begotten Son. I am the one!

To recognize the truth of the gospel in faith means to have one's eyes open to see God. Where can God be found? Of all those who have sought God throughout the history of humanity, who has indeed found God? So many in our age are tired of the search and resentful of the human resources that have been used, and abused, in conducting it. In a strange way, the gospel agrees; the search for God—including the Christian search—can finally lead only to the outer limits of the human self. Faith comes to recognize that God has sought *us* out, and found *us*. Faith views the cross and says, in an act of indescribable fulfillment: Yes, there You are. Now I see.

The barrier to this recognition of self and God in Christ is, then, not secularity or the supposed conflict between faith and reason. Faith is not credulity, asking us to believe something "higher" than reason, such as the world of the supernatural. The barrier to faith is *offense* at what we see when we recognize God and the self in the cross of Jesus Christ. Believing in the supernatural is easy compared to this opening of the eyes. Believing in nothing at all is child's play compared to the scandal of the cross. It is no wonder that the supposed battle between faith and reason is so often played out on the margins of Christianity, and should perhaps better be considered not a Christian concern at all, but a concern of "theism." At any rate, while the natural and the supernatural battle it out, over and against both is the gospel of redeeming love. Do not be offended by it; open your eyes!

In Jesus Christ, God became what we are, in order that we might become as he is. Faith is an echo of this exchange in the turning point from the old world of sin to the new world of the kingdom. In biblical language, faith is repentance. Repentance is a turning around, a leaving behind and a moving in a new direction. Again, faith is not an added dimension to the self, so much as it is a new self, a fresh start from the beginning.

What is left behind is the old self, held captive by the power of the old world. To use the language of Paul, it is the flesh, meaning not the physical body per se but the person, insofar as we are held captive to the desire to resist God and bless ourselves at all costs. When we come in faith to recognize God's redemption in Jesus Christ as God's redemption of us, we suddenly see ourselves in a new light. Truths are told that we may not even have been aware of ourselves, and have certainly sought to suppress if we do know them. Depths of the power of evil in our lives are brought to the surface for our troubled inspection. The closer we get to the cross, the more we see in ourselves what brought him there: the pride and anger, the hatred and egotism, the prejudices and hypocrisy, the idolatry and lust, the dominance of others and abuse of self.

More than that, the hearing of the gospel in faith manifests in us our fundamental hatred of grace. When we hear in faith the divine offer of forgiveness, we begin to see just how much we desire to make our own way, to prove ourselves worthy, to do it on our own. We are exposed as those who will not be helped, even by a loving God.

The turning around of faith, then, is first of all repentance of our sin. It is saying no to that in my life which corresponds to what God says no to on the cross of Jesus. We say no by acknowledging that we are sinners. That is, we learn to recognize the features of the old person in our thoughts, our words, our actions. We say no by confessing that we are sinners. God forgives our sin in order that we might approach him, even as sinners, without fear. Confession of sin is an honest declaration of who we are, without fear. What a strange occurrence! Where else in life can we summon up an honest declaration of who we are without fear? The true believer knows the exhilarating feeling of such fearless honesty. Finally, we say no to sin by renouncing its power. Through the power of the Spirit, we overcome the power of sin in our lives, and seek to overcome the power of sin and evil whenever we meet it. The addiction to sin is broken.

Repentance in faith is a turning point; it is not only a turning away from sin, but a turning toward something. That something is freedom. Faith is freedom in the Spirit of God. In faith, we are set on a new direction in life, a direction opened up for us by the redemption of God in Jesus Christ.

The new direction of life in faith is a process of leaving behind the power of sin and embracing the freedom of the Spirit. It is a process, not an adherence to a set of moral standards. Becoming a Christian does not mean suddenly finding a system of absolute truths and absolute moral values by which to guide one's life and by which to judge any and every ethical situation. It is not that the Christian life is somehow less certain, less definitive than such a system; rather, it is more certain, more definitive. I need a system of absolute truths and values because I lack confidence in my power to judge what is right and wrong. But the gospel proclaims that I have been delivered from the power of sin and evil and made new by the power of the Spirit. I am now who I am in a new relationship to God; and in this new relationship to God that now enlivens my life, I do not judge what is right and wrong; such judgment has been taken out of my hands by the judgment of God on the cross of Jesus. In its place comes a new person, ready to walk along the new path of freedom.

Every Christian is freed by the power of the Spirit to walk along the path of freedom. There is no system of absolute values to measure this path. However, new life in the Spirit is not amorphous and arbitrary. Freedom in the Spirit is not capriciousness, not self-will; it is a new will. Because the self is born anew in relationship to the Spirit of God in Christ, the new person has a very definite identity, a very definite goal. The Bible makes this point by speaking not of "laws" or "moral values" of the Spirit, but of the "fruit" of the Spirit. In freedom, this is the new person we become. "The fruit of the Spirit is love, joy, peace, patience, kindness, generosity, faithfulness, gentleness, and self-control. There is no law against such things" (Gal. 5:22–23). Believing in Christ means becoming this person. It does not mean setting out to do these things; these are not things to do, not rules to follow, not works to perform. "Works" are of the flesh (Gal. 5:19); fruits are from the Spirit. There is therefore no such thing as an abstract Christian ethic; there are only Christian people walking along the path of spiritual freedom.

Faith in God through Jesus Christ is recognition of the truth of the gospel and repentance in the power of the Spirit. Finally, faith is trust in Christ. The believer is one who, upon hearing the word of forgiveness in the name of Jesus, comes to trust him. Trust in Christ is the answer to a question, or perhaps a hundred questions, that our lives seem to generate: questions about meaning and purpose, about guilt and shame, about mortality and the darkness of evil. When I trust Christ through the gospel of Jesus Christ, I find the answer that I am no longer my own, but God's. God's care and love for me have so surrounded my life, so overflowed the boundaries of self-love, that I willingly place my self in his hands.

I trust Christ when I accept what he has done for me in his death and resurrection as the final answer to my life. I can and do attempt to give my own answers: to answer the sense of guilt with renewed attempts at moral transformation; to face the question of meaning with some sense of purpose in family, or career, or values; to meet the feeling of helplessness with a stronger ego and sense of identity; to conquer my loneliness with efforts to connect with others. I trust Christ when I receive from *him* the answers to these questions as a gift. I do not simply stop asking the questions—Christians too seek forgiveness and purpose and a sense of self. Indeed, through the power of the cross Christians become even more aware of just how fragile our answers to these questions are. Trusting Christ means accepting, once for all as well as moment by moment, that the gift of God in Christ is freely given to me.

If I do not trust, I "work" for my salvation. I attempt to face my guilt through repeated efforts at moral transformation, in hope that someday these will be enough to merit the divine forgiveness. I strive to give meaning and purpose to my life so that it will not be wasted; I try to count for something in a world that seems to make that more and more difficult. I reach out in friendship and compassion to others in order to break down the walls that separate people. I want to make my life worth something, certainly to myself, but also to others, and to God—if there is such a reality. But where do such works lead? Am I not constantly made aware by such efforts of how helpless I really am? I take one step forward, and feel a sense of achievement, only to be pulled two steps backward, where I start all over again. Make no mistake, religion, and especially Christianity, can be used to provide me with just such an opportunity for works. I can be involved in "Christian" life and service in such a way that I am fundamentally attempting to justify myself before God and others. Far more effectively than so-called secular culture, the world of religion can conceal from me my own helplessness, my own guilt, my own finitude.

There is another kind of works, another alternative to faith, that seems to be flourishing in our own time. I can trust Christ, or I can work for my redemption—or, I can give up. Though it is often confused with faith, giving up is as contrary to the gospel as trying to earn my salvation. I give up when I face life with passive resignation. What does it matter who I am? I attempt to suppress the fact that I am personally accountable to God for my life. It seems better to accept my own helplessness; better to resign myself to the banality of evil and sin; better to protect myself as much as possible from feelings of guilt and shame, realizing that they are natural to human beings.

Myriad artificial worlds are available to us to protect and nourish the resigned self: the therapies that promise self-acceptance, the drugs that promote energy and escape, the television that offers a semblance of connectedness with others, and so forth. Again, the Christian religion is the worst culprit. Its language and liturgy can be and are used to conceal the resigned self from the truth of faith in the gospel. Saying yes to

Christ in faith gives me a new self; it both exposes and acts upon my accountability to God as Creator and Redeemer.

I trust Jesus Christ when I accept his answer to my life as my own answer for myself. It is neither partially active, as in works, nor partially passive, as in resignation. It is entirely active, because it generates a new life, and yet entirely passive, because it accepts that what I have comes entirely from the free grace of God. The one who trusts Christ knows the truth in this paradox. The active and passive self are one in the freedom of saying yes to God.

Christ is our righteousness before God by faith alone; we are justified by faith. Justification means being put in right relation to God, becoming righteous. As we have seen, the gospel proclaims that God wills human beings to live in relationship with himself. In the light of that proclamation, we have seen that human beings, and I myself, fall far short of the divine will for their lives. God wills me to be what I am not. Even if I may come in part to recognize this will, I seem unable and unwilling to become what I see to be the fulfillment of my life. But God, in his grace and mercy, became what we are—sinners under the power of evil—in order that we might become what he wills us to be—righteous. By faith I receive what in the grace of God is freely given to me: justification.

Faith justifies me before God because God is gracious, not because of the superior attractiveness of faith. When I trust Jesus Christ, I do not do something that somehow makes up for all the other sins I have committed. Faith is not a work—not an act that I perform for the sake of preserving or restoring my destiny and standing before God. Faith is opposed to works; I come to trust Christ only when I abandon all attempts at works.

Indeed, I am not justified by my faith; I am justified by the grace of God, which comes to me through my act of faith. My justification before God is not a goal that I will reach at the end of my days, once I have striven to be the best person I can be, relying on the mercy of God. My justification is what I already am because Jesus Christ, on the cross, took away the power and guilt of my sin and imputed to me his own righteousness. I strive throughout my life, in faith, hope, and love, to become what in Jesus Christ I already am. To trust God means to accept, joyfully and gratefully and full of wonder and adoration, the fact that God has already made things right with himself for me. "There is therefore now no condemnation for those who are in Christ Jesus" (Rom. 8:1). "He has rescued us from the power of darkness and transferred us into the kingdom of his beloved Son, in whom we have redemption, the forgiveness of sins" (Col. 1:13–14).

Let us be clear. We are not saying that God justifies me as I am in myself; what I am in myself has been brought to light in the story of Jesus. I am one who, along with the rest of humanity, handed Jesus over to be crucified through my sin. What I am in myself is what Jesus becomes on the cross: a judged sinner. No, God does not justify me for what I am in myself, but rather judges what I am in myself in his judgment of Jesus on Calvary. Neither does God justify me for what I might become, even as a Christian. The gospel does not proclaim that Jesus died in order to give me a second chance at meriting divine justification through a more worthy Christian life. The gospel proclaims that God justifies me freely by his grace through the life, death, and resurrection of Jesus Christ. To be justified by faith means to receive the free gift of salvation; and even as I receive it, I know that my receiving is itself the gift of the Spirit. To be a Christian means to be willingly surrounded, from beginning to end, by the marvelous love of God made real for us in Jesus Christ our Lord.

Love

"YOU SHALL love the Lord your God with all your heart, and with all your soul, and with all your strength, and with all your mind; and your neighbor as yourself" (Luke 10:27). This love is the new direction our life takes when we become a Christian. This love is the will of God for human life made real and possible for us in the power of the Spirit. Through faith in the gospel of Jesus Christ I am justified before God; through love, I strive to become what by faith I already am.

Becoming a Christian means a lifelong relationship of love to God. It is not an extension of my capacity to love others; indeed, as we shall see, loving others will become an extension of my new capacity to love God. Love for God is a new capacity because I stand before God in a way that I am unable to stand before others. I am completely without fear, in the human sense of fear. I do not fear God because he has proven himself entirely reliable in his dealings with his creatures. The figure of Jesus dead on the cross and risen from the grave is fixed indelibly in my mind. In him is the God I love, the God who proclaims his love to me. With him I am safe. Neither do I fear that something else will disrupt my love of God. For what is there that can finally withstand the turning of God in love toward humanity, and toward me? There can certainly at times *seem* to be such; but again, the image of the crucified and risen Jesus conquers all doubt. Nor do I fear myself in my relationship to God. There is nothing in myself of which I fear exposure. All has been exposed, even depths of sin and evil that I did not, and certainly may still not, know. As strange as it sounds, I am able to love God without fear because I have been judged by God. There is nothing left to hide, even if I wanted to. Indeed, this realization is the true fear of God.

To love God is to respond to his love for me with all my intellect, will, and feelings. We find this love pictured in the psalms, the sense of utter devotion and enjoyment in the presence of Almighty God. Through prayer I speak to him; through meditation on the Word I listen to him; through the life of obedience I honor him. I love God by entering into the relationship that he himself has established through Christ in the power of the Spirit. The relationship is an end in itself; it has no use, to me or to God, beyond itself. To love God, then, means to seek this companionship with God for its own sake, not for some need. To do so is therefore without necessity; it is the highest act of human freedom.

I love God by accepting his good for my life. Through Jesus Christ, God has determined the good for every creature whom he loves. Christ has fulfilled the Law and the Prophets; that is, he has, in a definitive way, once for all manifested the will of God for human life. The Christian finds himself or herself no longer held captive by the counterfeit images of human life by which humanity is held hostage. The Christian is the one who, on being freed from bondage, desires nothing but to strive for the image of humanity revealed in Christ. To love God is to obey his will. It is to find in the will of God for human life the only possible road on which to travel.

What is the will of God for human life revealed in the gospel of Jesus Christ? The Bible answers this very simply: just as Jesus Christ established relationship between God and humanity by giving himself for our sake, so too we who believe in him must seek to establish relationship with others by giving of ourselves for their sake. To follow the will of God revealed in Jesus Christ is to love our neighbor.

Love for my neighbor accepts my neighbor on the same basis that I am accepted by God. I accept my neighbor as a forgiven and justified sinner, as one for whom Christ died and rose again and whom he seeks to bring into the fellowship of the new world of God. I love, I do not judge; if I judge, I exercise a prerogative that has been taken out of my hands through the suffering of Jesus. Indeed, I cannot love and judge, for I would thereby expose the fact that I do not love my neighbor with the full acceptance I myself receive. Judgment goes together with the righteousness of works; full acceptance in love goes together with the righteousness of faith.

Notice that the will of God in human life is love for *neighbor*, not "universal love" of humanity. The latter is a product of the Enlightenment and needs criticism in the light of the biblical witness. Love of neighbor is always a concrete, specific act of help to one who is in need. As in the parable of the good Samaritan, the neighbor is the one whom I find in need, indeed the one whom I almost stumble onto as I live my life. I love my neighbor when I discover his or her need and respond with real help. As Jesus said, I love when I feed the hungry, give drink to the thirsty, clothe the naked, heal the sick, visit the prisoner. Compared to such concrete acts of love, the ideal of "universal love" seems hardly meaningful.

But who is my neighbor? In a strange way, this is perhaps the burning issue of our time for the Christian life. The fact is that, for reasons of culture and social-economic development, we are simply unaware of our neighbor. Our lives are terribly isolated from the lives of others; and even those we do meet, we meet only for a specific purpose, such as at the workplace, or in impersonal exchanges, such as a trip to the store. When we are not at work or performing the tasks of daily life, whom do we see? Who is really our neighbor? More than that, on the rare occasions that we meet others beyond such impersonal relationships, we tend, at best, to gather with others exactly like ourselves. Anyone who has attended an American church will know what this is like; even in the community of faith, we come together only with others like us. Are such people really our neighbors? Is not part of the parable of the good Samaritan the sense of *distance* that is overcome when this human being reaches over to that other, very different human being? The Christian life in our time must begin with *making connections* with others, especially those who are different from ourselves. Only then will we see the need of our neighbor and be able to respond as best we can. We are separated from our neighbor just as surely as we were separated from God through our sin. So now we must be reconciled through finding and making connections with our neighbor, just as God has been reconciled to us through finding and making connections with us.

Love for neighbor means seeing our neighbors for who they really are, in their need. Ours is a society in which help is offered based only on the perspective of the helper, not on the actual need of those we attempt to love. We attempt to love by participating in causes. We discern the need of our neighbor through the application of some ideological perspective. More often than not, we offer help in the form of programs, or support of programs, designed to address their needs. Step by step we then become further removed from the actual lives of those around us. Though some causes and programs may well benefit some people, they cannot be an effective substitute for the claim of God on human life. That claim means direct, immediate action in response to direct, intimate contact with those we meet along the way.

Christian love sees our neighbor as a human being, not as the function of some cause. It is a realistic love, a love in contact with the reality of its object, not an ideological love, in which those whom we love become the means to the end of a fulfilled vision of human society. The gospel of Jesus Christ teaches no ideology; it offers

no specific political programs, no economic or social system, no "ism" of any kind. It is not that the gospel is
not concerned about what we call political, economic,
and social issues; we shall see in the next chapter that it
is vitally concerned.[2] But the gospel calls the followers
of Jesus Christ to address the human beings with whom
each of us comes into contact as specific people in specific, concrete circumstances. Whether or not an economic program will solve the problem of the poverty of
my neighbor, I am called to give him or her money.
Whether or not prison reform will better the condition
of our prisoners, I am called to direct concern in caring
for a prisoner. Whether or not the problem of racism will
be solved in our courts and in our culture, I am called to
friendship and solidarity with my white neighbor or my
black neighbor. Christian love is not an "ism"—it is
direct action.

Concrete acts of love to my neighbor are possible
only when I see my neighbors in their real need. That is
only possible when who I am has been transformed by
the power of the Spirit. We have so far spoken of love as
action, and that is consistent with the biblical emphasis.
But love is not something I do as opposed to something
I am. It is something I can do because of who I have
become in the freedom of the gospel. How difficult it is
simply to see others for who they are in their real need!
Even supposedly loving acts of heroic proportions are
often only possible because our neighbor fits into the
categories of what the self is able and willing to give. As
often as not, what pass for acts of love simply pass right
by the real need of our neighbor. We do not see them,
because our eyes are lamps by which the self defines its

vision. In the freedom of the Spirit, they become mirrors of reality.

Two biblical concepts characterize the self freed by the Spirit to love others: patience and kindness. Patience is the ability to withhold judgment for the sake of understanding. The natural self champs at the bit of judgment; it feels that it cannot act until it understands, and it cannot understand until it judges the situation. It is imprisoned by its own need to judge. The patient self waits for the neighbor to declare himself or herself; one listens, one inquires, one stands by the neighbor, and therefore one's action means something to the neighbor and not simply to oneself.

The loving self is also kind. One does not compare a neighbor with some ideal standard of humanity, tucked away somewhere in one's brain. One accepts the neighbor in his or her own finite and, yes, sinful reality. Ideal standards of humanity are simply projections of a self eager to prove itself worthy. Though Christian elements may be mixed in, they are in fact a foreign substance; Jesus nowhere teaches, nor does he act consistently with, the idea that we can approach others with an ideal human person in mind.

How rare such patience and kindness are! Where can they truly be found? Where do we see acts of love coming from a patient and kind heart? From whence comes a sincere and honest love of neighbor? Only when a sense of the grace of God has transformed our very heart, only then will our action, our tone of voice, our very face manifest the love that God gives.

The way of love is the way of the cross. When we love others in the power of the Spirit of Christ, which is the power of the new world of the kingdom of God, we love with that love with which Jesus loved us. He loved us by giving himself for our sake; we therefore must love others by giving ourselves for their sake. True love does not "insist on its own way" (1 Cor. 13:5); that is, it makes a person so rich that there is nothing else left to be sought for the self. There remains only what can be given away.

The way of the cross is denial of self for the sake of others. This does not mean the disappearance of the self, or the loss of identity through dependence on, or dominance by, others. Self-denial is not codependence. I can exercise self-denial only when my self has been rescued from bondage to sin and evil, including the destructiveness of dependence as an enslavement to others. Self-denial means that I come into full possession of myself only when I realize that I am not my own, but God's. There is nothing more affirming and liberating than this realization. No amount of self-affirmation and self-esteem can compare with coming to know and trust that we are not our own, but God's creatures—not some god in general, but *this* God, who died and rose again for our sake. It is for this reason that we love through self-denial: for in doing so, we are coming to be like God. We are finding our lives through him, learning to love as he loves.

There are no Christian ethics, no system of absolute moral truths, higher than this love through self-denial. Becoming a Christian means entering a lifelong path of learning to love as God loves through fellowship with Christ. Becoming a Christian means daily learning new ways to exercise this love in our life situations. Stumbling as a Christian means momentarily forgetting the image of the cross, or perhaps returning to the bondage of the self to its own destructive desire to fulfill itself. The point is this: Learning to exercise Christian love through self-denial is not a matter of acquiring a specific new set of behaviors. It is rather a matter of acquiring a new capacity to discern, in each new situation, how to love as God loves. We must hold nothing back; not our pleasures, our convenience, our time, our wealth, our reputation, even our very lives. All must be placed into the service of learning to love as God loves. We can do so without fear because we know and trust that God is a gentle and kind teacher, who wills only to enrich our lives with true fulfillment.

Love abides. We are not now all that we can be; but when we love, we already are what we shall be. We are not now all that we can be: though citizens of the new world by the grace of God, we are held back by sin and evil. God gives us the freedom to participate fully in the kingdom, but which of us makes full use of that freedom? We trust with all our heart the forgiveness of God proclaimed in the gospel; yet it is seldom easy to see how that forgiveness works itself out in our lives. We trust, because we cannot know. Nevertheless, when we love, we already are what we shall be. Learning to love as God loves makes us into the people that we shall become in the coming kingdom of God. It gives to our lives eternal significance. We cannot now see the big picture, the full glory of God's plan for the world in Jesus Christ. But a life of love is a life that will endure forever.

Hope

IN FAITH, I already am righteous before God, accepted by him, and brought into the new world of the kingdom of God. In love, I become what I already am, making real in my life the claim of God on all those who call upon his name. The Christian life is about what I am by faith, and about what I become in love. It is also about what I am yet to be. According to the gospel of Jesus Christ, being a Christian means living in hope for what I am yet to be. It is not a different kind of life, nor a different faith, nor a different Christ from the one known through faith and love. I hope because of who I am, and who I become. Nevertheless, I am not fully embracing the gospel until my life takes on the character of Christian hope, just as surely as I become one who believes and one who loves.

What do I hope for as a Christian? Do I not already have all that I need in Jesus Christ? To be sure, the call to hope does not compromise the fact that God is already my redeemer through the cross and resurrection of Jesus Christ. Jesus came into the world to save lost sinners, and that he did on Calvary. However, the Bible also testifies that those who believe in the gospel of redemption look forward in hope to an as yet undisclosed time, a consummation which is to come. It is precisely those whose eyes are fixed on the cross of Christ, and who witness the empty tomb, who know that this same Christ has in store for the world something that is yet to be revealed. That is what the Christian looks for in hope.

What is this something? When the Bible testifies to this reality, it uses a different kind of language from its more ordinary prose and poetry and narrative. It uses a kind of picture language, laced through with symbolic images. The picture language of the New Testament hope means, on the one hand, that I cannot know this future in the way that I know my own past, my present, or even my attempts to project my own future. It is not my future, but a new age altogether. In the wisdom of God, we have not been given a detailed description—or else we could perhaps come to predict this future. On the other hand, the picture language of the Bible does mean that we have an image of this world to come. As Barth put it, it is not the night in which all cows are gray; it has color, and contour, and depth. Though I cannot predict it, I am led by Holy Scripture to imagine it, to long for it, to live my life as if it is ultimately more real than the world that I do know.

What I hope for is a change, a transformation, but a transformation in which the end of the process is not at all contained in the beginning. Like any transformation, there will be some continuity; though I will be changed, it will still be I myself who am there in the coming kingdom; though the world will be transformed, it will still be this creation of God, not an alternative universe. In this transformation, the continuity is *not* because what is new is somehow already contained in what is old—not, that is, because I contain in myself some capacity for life in the coming kingdom, or that the world is like the acorn, which can grow into the mighty oak. The continuity comes from the *promise* of God alone. When I hope as a Christian I cannot look to myself, or to the world around, for the content of my hope; I can look only to the promise of God.

Let us consider more closely what kind of life a life of hope is. It is first of all a life in which the coming kingdom of God is considered ultimately more real than the old world of sin and evil. In hope, I realize that good and evil are not equal combatants on the world stage, struggling for domination over the minds and lives of human beings. Through faith in the crucified and risen Jesus, I realize in hope that evil is that which is passing away, which indeed has already been disarmed on the cross. It lingers to corrupt our hearts and foul our world, but it does so as the impotent rage of a defeated enemy. Evil is dead, and reaches out to grab us only as that which is already perishing.

The good is not some capacity found in me or anyone else to withstand evil and build a livable world. Hope means the realization that "the good" is the almighty power of God who, in Jesus Christ, has established a new world of righteousness and peace and truth.

To live in Christian hope means to live in the light of the coming kingdom of God in the midst of this perishing world. It does not mean to escape this perishing world, as the unfortunate ascetic movements in Christian history would argue. Even if it were possible somehow to leave the world behind, perhaps through forms of abstinence or self-flagellation, it would mean no longer living in hope; for hope is always invested in something yet to be. Asceticism attempts to convert hope into *possession*, and therefore loses it altogether. Nor does hope mean to live in resignation in this perishing world, as if the coming kingdom of God were merely a distant goal for which we must wait passively, or perhaps merely an idealistic construct of the human imagination. I live in this world, but I live in hope only if I live for the coming kingdom of God.

As Paul states it, living in hope means living "as though" (1 Cor. 7:25-31); as though what I own means nothing to me in light of the treasures of the kingdom; as though my marriage and my relationships with others are open to the new human community of God; as though my dealings with others are obliged to reflect the new world of God. Hope means a personal ethics in which the claims of the kingdom of God are more true to me than the more obvious common sense of this perishing world. The Sermon on the Mount is just such a call to hope; I turn the other cheek, for example, because I live in confidence that the day is coming soon when I will not be hurt nor will I hurt. I pray for and love my enemies as though they were my closest friends, not because I close my eyes to the realities of the world, but because I live in confidence that one day soon there will be no enemy.

There is a negative side to hope. The believer is one who knows that the coming kingdom of God is more powerful and far greater than the reality of this passing world. I therefore see the world in which we live in the light of the new world of God. What I see is the goodness of God's creation, but also the terrible evil and injustice of this world. Hope exposes evil; it brings to light what people without hope simply cannot see. People without hope in the gospel cannot understand that true Christian hope is not a flight from this world; indeed, it opens the eyes to the realization of this world with clarity and understanding, because it sets our knowledge of this world against the true backdrop of our imagination of the world to come. I know this world because in hope I can imagine the new world.

Hope therefore means an active renunciation of evil, a struggle against the forces of sin and wickedness which afflict and oppress the human community. Once again, hope only seems paradoxical on the surface, while underlying it is the most certain logic. I struggle against evil, not because I believe that somehow my struggle will win over the forces of darkness. The purpose of my struggle is not to defeat evil. By faith I know that evil has already been defeated on the cross. In fact, my struggle against evil has no real purpose or context broader than itself. It is not part of a grand design for the moral progress of the human community, or for the final attainment of world peace. My hope is my confidence that an infinitely better world is God's design for our world. My struggle, therefore, is simply what it is: my own attempt, by myself and with others, to fight against evil wherever I find it, in order freely to serve God and joyfully to love and serve others. I do not measure my struggle by its function in the grand design of human progress. Those who do so will sooner or later abandon the struggle, for who can really fathom such progress? Who can really imagine such a design? The struggle of Christian hope against evil may or may not mean solidarity with this or that cause, this or that activist organization. Yet the believer always knows what the real point of it all is. God's design for the world, which we can now only imagine in hope, is far greater than any conceivable human design and far more liberating to honest and fruitful and lasting human involvement in service to others.

There is a positive side to hope in Christ as well, a side so powerful that it can change the very character of the Christian, the way a person experiences the world and his or her place in it. The one who hopes comes, through that hope, to have courage. The courage of the Christian is not heroic, at least not in the sense that is portrayed in fiction and popular culture. There the hero battles against insurmountable odds until, quite unexpectedly, the hero turns things to his or her own favor. The hero wins in the end because of mastering the elements of the game and finally beating the odds, either through cunning or through overwhelming force.

Christian courage is not like that. It is not the courage of the hero, nor does it bring a hero's destiny. First of all, the courage that comes from hope in the gospel does not see the enemy to be overcome as some alien invader out there which threatens the community. The enemy is myself. Whatever the world does to harm me, I deserve far worse as a rebel against God. As I look on the cross of Jesus Christ, as a witness to his suffering for my sake, suddenly all other suffering is surrounded and embraced by his hands, nailed to the cross. I am a sinner, who deserves what he suffered; therefore nothing that can happen to me can outweigh what he delivered me from by his death on the cross for my sake.

Moreover the courage of the Christian gets a reward different from that of the hero. The hero, in the end, wins the prize that was sought all along—riches, or fame, or love. But the Christian does not get what he or she wants. In fact, through hope in the gospel I come to realize that what I want is nothing compared to what God wants for me. Hope means the confidence that

God's promise is far more certain, and filled with far greater abundance, than what I can have and want for myself. I can face whatever life has to offer me, for good or ill, because I know that a day is coming when God will offer me riches beyond compare.

That does not mean that my life now is somehow unimportant, or is merely transitional to an eternal future. That would not be courage so much as simple escapism. I have one life, one opportunity to do what I can to make something out of the place and time in which I find myself, with the skills and capacities I bring with me. How can I make it count when the cards seem stacked against me? There are illness and tragedy and deep pain; I lack the wisdom I need, the resources I desire, the strength that others seem to possess. There are missed opportunities for love, and in the end there is death all around—of others about whom I care, and finally of myself. How can I live?

Through Jesus Christ I have courage to live my life. Through faith I trust that he has already delivered me from the bondage of guilt and the judgment of death. Through love I seek to transform the elements of my life into connections with others, at the same time helping them and finding new life for myself. Most importantly here, through hope I affirm that God will make of my life something far greater than I can yet imagine. As the psalmist says in his prayers:

> You have kept count of my tossings;
>   put my tears in your bottle.
>   Are they not in your record?

>   (Ps. 56:8)

My suffering is not removed from the presence of God; indeed, in the light of the cross, is it not my suffering that is closest to God? Neither my life nor my death, my sorrow nor my joy, is scattered to the winds in an uncertain play of forces. They are all in his hand. And he will fulfill his gracious purpose. Courage!

Biblical Texts for Consideration

Faith

Psalm 32
Mark 1:14–15
Acts 2
Romans 4; 8; 10
1 Corinthians 2
2 Corinthians 5:16–21
Galatians 2:19–21
Galatians 5
Ephesians 3:14–19

Hope

Psalm 42, 56
Ephesians 5:15-20
1 Thessalonians 5:1-11
Hebrews 11
Revelation 2-3; 21-22

Love

Matthew 22:34-40
Matthew 25:31-46
Luke 10:25-37
1 Corinthians 13
Ephesians 4-6
Colossians 3:1-17
James 2
James 4:11–12

6

THE GOSPEL AND THE HUMAN COMMUNITY

THOSE WHO are redeemed by God to live lives of faith, love, and hope do not live alone. On the one hand, they are invited by the Spirit of God to companionship with others who know and trust the gospel of Jesus Christ; that is, they are invited to full participation in the Christian church. On the other hand, they continue to live, not only in the world that God has created, but in the world that human beings have created; that is, they live in the world of human culture. We must complete our study of the theology of the gospel with some reflections on the participation of the Christian in these two communities. Finally, we shall conclude our study with some reflections on the gospel and the future.

The Gospel in the Church

THE CHRISTIAN is not alone; he or she is invited by God to share in the company of those whose eyes have been opened to the truth of the gospel in the death and resurrection of Jesus Christ. It is a vast company, a company that transcends and transforms the boundaries of race, of nation, of class, of gender. It is a company that seeks among its members to represent, in a provisional way, the redeemed humanity that is to come. Most of all, it is a company that seeks to bear witness to the world of the good news of the redemption of the world in Jesus Christ. This company lives to make this witness.

The Christian is invited to join a company that is at the same time united by its faith and yet wonderfully diverse in the humanity it represents. In this company I will find others with faith like my own, but I will not find only others like myself. The Bible describes this company as a body, indeed, the body of Christ. It is one body, and therefore in some sense a unity; and yet it has many parts, and therefore is in a profound sense diverse.

Let us consider first the unity of the church. "There is one body and one Spirit, just as you were called to the one hope of your calling, one Lord, one faith, one baptism, one God and Father of all, who is above all and through all and in all" (Eph. 4:4-6). What makes this company of human beings a true fellowship is not the similarity of the people who are present in it. Rather, its unity comes from the one Lord who breathes life into it and nourishes it. If it is not God's people, it is not the true church. If it is God's people, because God is one Lord, the church must be in a profound sense a united company of faith and life. I do not *see* this unity, if by that I mean recognizing every other Christian as somehow like myself; but I must *believe* this unity, in that I recognize in every sister and brother of Jesus Christ the same faith in the same gospel.

Of course, what I do see is the sad fact of Christian fragmentation, Christian schism, Christian disharmony. I see modern denominations, whose origins from the sixteenth century to the present have often enough been the attempt to convert the unity of the church based on faith into the false unity of the church built on the similarity of human beings. To be sure, the existence of Christian denominations has in its own way been a testimony to the diversity of the people of God; but are they so any longer? Do Christian denominations continue to bear witness to the richness of God's grace, or do they not, rather, betray the sad fact of stubbornness and pride and jealousy among Christian people? Who is not appalled by the fact that denominations tend to attract similar people, and therefore close the eyes and hearts of Christian people to the true diversity of the church, and therefore to the true unity as well?

Jesus Christ, as he is attested for us in Holy Scripture, is the unity of the church. The Bible itself is a unity in diversity; it gives to the church a language of faith which gathers people into one belief and yet frees us for a diversity in living that faith. Whatever draws away from the unity of faith in Jesus Christ attested in Holy Scripture is schism. We do not need a new universal denomination, or a universal church constitution, or a universal church government, or a universal church confession. What we need for the unity of the church we already have—the gospel of Christ.

We give thanks also for the rich diversity of the church, given by the richness of the Spirit of God. The diversity is not contrary to the unity; indeed, it is made possible by it. Without the unity of the gospel in the church, the diversity would be, and so often is, chaos. Without the unity of the gospel there is only strife, dissension, jealousy, self-seeking, and finally open and unbridgeable schism. But in the unity of the gospel the church of Jesus Christ is blessed by the Spirit of God with luxuriant riches beyond measure.

The Spirit of God empowers every Christian with a particular skill in service of the kingdom of God. This skill is a gift from God; it is an opportunity to contribute freely to the living work of Jesus Christ in the world. According to the Bible there are many such gifts from the Spirit of God in the church: there are teachers, pastors, evangelists, activists; there are those who pray constantly, those who give greater amounts of money, those who attend to the needs of the sick and the dying; there are those who sing, those who cook, those who clean. All live by the same faith, the same love, the same hope. Yet all live out this faith, love, and hope in a different way. No one Christian is an adequate representation of the body of Christ. While each is a witness to Christ, the full witness of the church depends on the multifarious contribution of its diverse members.

What a great gift this is from God! Yet how sad it is that it is so little appreciated. Where the gospel of God's free grace is not cherished as the very center of the church's life, the diverse gifts of the Spirit become the special interests of its competing members. Without the unity of the gospel, each member uses the special gift of God entrusted to him or her as a measure for the true Christian life, a measure by which to judge the contribution of others.

Moreover, the diversity of the church is based on the fact that in the church the walls that separate human beings are torn down. The company of believers is a harmony in Christ. The gospel of God's justifying grace in Christ tears down the walls of gender; it tears down the walls of prejudice; it tears down the walls of social class; it tears down the walls of nationalism. And yet, here again, how devastating to the church is the fact that these walls are so often rebuilt—in the church! Walls of race, of gender, of class, of nation are erected on the very spot where only ruins remained from the victory of Christ on the cross. We mock him when we allow these walls. And we lose the tremendous benefit of life as the body of Christ.[1]

What is the purpose of the church? Why is there such a company as those who comprise the body of Christ? Why the varied gifts of the Spirit, and the inclusive humanity the Spirit engenders? Our reflections on the meaning of the gospel of God's redemption shed significant light on these questions. The church can be viewed in many different ways, theological as well as nontheological, such as sociological or political. The argument here, however, is that unless the church is viewed in the light of the gospel of redemption, the true purpose of the church can be ignored or misconstrued. The true purpose? Is there such a thing? Yes indeed; for if not, the church has long since lost its right to exist as a justifiable human institution. Unless it is upheld by the purpose of the grace of God revealed in the gospel, the church is at best a highly ambiguous moral force in society, and at worst—and it has often been at worst—a self-seeking and arrogant association no different from

169

the other social organizations with which it competes. What is the true purpose of the church? In the light of the gospel, we cannot pass this question by.

We can begin with a comprehensive answer: the church exists as a provisional representation of redeemed humanity through faith in the crucified and risen Lord. In the company of believers there is realized a new humanity; it is certainly not of its own making, for in themselves the company of believers are poor lost sinners, no different from the world. Not in themselves, but by faith in the righteousness of Jesus Christ, and in the power of the Spirit of God, the members of the church are reborn as citizens of the new world of the kingdom of God. They live here, in this world, still plagued by the power of evil; but their true citizenship, their fundamental loyalty and innermost being, is transferred to the new world of God.

Members of the body of Christ do not enjoy participation in the kingdom of God as if it separates them from the rest of humanity. As a true Christian, I will never draw a line between myself and the world, for I know that Jesus Christ has already drawn such a line—between himself and the whole of humanity, including me. The true Christian in the true church participates in the body of Christ as one who wishes to represent, to stand in for, those who are outside the church. In every act of faith, love, and hope, I act not only for myself, but on behalf of those whose eyes have not, or not yet, been opened. I do so because I believe the promise of the gospel of God, who desires that all should be saved and come to the knowledge of the truth.

The church fulfills its purpose by engaging in a twofold mission, an inner mission and an outer mission.

Both aspects of the mission of the church are crucial to the fulfillment of its purpose. It cannot neglect one aspect and yet be good in the other; they stand or fall together.

The inner mission of the church is, first of all, the praise and worship and glorification of God. Through its hymns it sings praises to God. Through its prayers it offers him thanks and praise, and calls upon him for help. Through its preaching it bears witness to his word and through its sacraments embraces his promise. Through its teaching it seeks to expand and confirm its insights into the revelation of God. The church gathers weekly, not first of all to maintain its own identity, but simply to devote itself again and again to the service of God. Redemption means a covenant fulfilled, a relationship with Almighty God. The church exists to celebrate and enjoy this relationship, and in so doing to establish its own reality in the relationship.

Just as the individual Christian can come to *use* God rather than *enjoy* God (Augustine), so the church can employ God rather than praise and honor him. The church employs God when it takes for granted what God provides, as if it is God's "business" to create, to redeem, to nourish. The church employs God when it calls upon him primarily to underwrite its own causes, especially causes in the name of Christianity. In how many services of Christian worship is the name of God used frequently for this or that request, this or that idea, this or that program, and yet not at all used to thank and praise and worship him? to ask him, really ask him, for help in specific prayer requests, as if we really believe that he will help? One wonders if the Christian churches have not altogether lost this sense of being the company of believers addressing God face to face in worship. It is a simple task, built on the simplest of faiths—but where is it performed?

The inner mission of the church is furthermore the cultivation of a fellowship of love among those who follow Jesus Christ. The church is, as we have seen, an inclusive and varied company of people united in the gospel of redemption. However, it does not simply *exist* in this way. The mission of the church is that believers come to appreciate and love those who are different from themselves in the body of Christ. "Toleration" has no part in the Christian church; if I can do no more than tolerate, I have not found the love of God. I cherish my brothers and sisters; I respect their individual life experiences, and seek to learn from them; I enjoy and appreciate them, because I have been freed by God from the self-imposed task of judging them.

It is unfortunate that there is a tendency to think of "churches" as denominational superstructures and large, impersonal organizations such as the television ministries. The church is the company of believers gathered in a specific place, at a specific time, to worship God and cultivate a fellowship of love. It is local; names are known, personal greetings exchanged, specific needs met. Perhaps there was a time for a worldwide "Christendom," as in the Middle Ages, and for the large, bureaucratically controlled denominations, functioning like small nation-states in the modern period; but has not the time come for a concentrated revival of the local church? The point is not to withdraw one's attention and interest from the church of God throughout the world.

The point is, rather, to *act* to form an authentic fellowship of love in the worship of God, not simply to speak of it in liturgy and theology.

The church fulfills its purpose of being a provisional representation of redeemed humanity through an outer mission as well, a responsibility beyond the walls of the company of believers. A text from the Gospel of Matthew will make the point simply: "Go therefore and make disciples of all nations, baptizing them in the name of the Father and of the Son and of the Holy Spirit, and teaching them to obey everything that I have commanded you" (Matt. 28:19–20). The mission of the church beyond its walls is to bear witness to the gospel of Jesus Christ, and through that witness to participate in God's gathering of all human beings to himself. If it neglects that mission, it not only loses its identity, not only fails its obligation to God, it likewise fails its obligation to those who are not members of the company of believers. Every member of the body of Christ knows that only the grace of God has opened our eyes to the redemption that is ours in the cross of Christ. Every Christian therefore sees everyone outside the company of believers as one like oneself and on whom God wills his grace to shine. To neglect the opportunity to testify to that grace is to neglect everything.

Now, it is certainly true that the church, by its very nature, moves in many directions in its relation to the world. It works for peace and justice, contributes to the poor, helps to feed the hungry, and so much more. These are works of love, commanded by Jesus Christ to those who follow him. But we must not take back with the left hand what we have just given with the right;

the primary mission of the church, without which it becomes lifeless and irrelevant, is witness to the gospel of Jesus Christ, who died for the sins of the world.

What do we mean by witness? We mean testimony to the word of God; we mean telling the story of Jesus Christ crucified and risen again for the redemption of human beings; we mean communication of the gospel. The growth of this witness is the history of the church; the diminution of this witness is the decay of the church. Granted, there is no doubt that those outside the church will benefit from the works of love performed by Christians throughout the world. Likewise, those outside the church may be attracted to the gospel through more than simple declarations—through, for instance, the life example of mature and devoted Christians, or through being shown the love of God by the care of a Christian. But again, we must not misjudge here; if the church is not declaring the gospel near and far whatever the works that accompany it, it is failing its responsibility to those outside the company of believers.

Why does this proclamation matter so much? Why select only one aspect of the church as its central mission to the world? The commission of Christ is the main answer, and it stands on its own. It also makes sense, for whatever works of love we can perform, we are enabled by him; whatever sense of justice we experience and fight for, we receive from his commandment; whatever urging we feel to work for peace comes from his reconciliation, and his claim on our lives. Without him we can do nothing that really matters for the welfare of our neighbor. In that light, it makes sense that the primary thing we can give our neighbor is Jesus himself. We cannot, of course, open his eyes to the truth of the gospel, for that is God's alone to do. But God has entrusted us with nothing less than the message of God's redemption; to proclaim it to another is to give the best that we can give.

The Gospel and Human Culture

THROUGH THE grace of the gospel of Jesus Christ, the Christian is free to participate in the company of believers, the church. At the same time, Christians must also live in the world (Where else can they go?) which includes the world of human culture. How are Christians to get along in the world knowing, as they do, that the coming kingdom of God is the only hope? What light does the gospel shed on human culture, which includes the realm of politics, art, education, economics, entertainment, leisure, and more?

The gospel is the ultimate truth about human life. Not our reflections on the gospel, but the person of Jesus Christ himself, crucified and risen for our sake, is the truth about all human life and every individual life. Every other truth is only relative in the light of the ultimate truth of the gospel. Every other truth is radically relativized in juxtaposition with the absolute truth of the gospel of redemption. Relative truths do not endure; they come and go, attracting human attention and admiration for a time, then passing away to the attention only of historians. The realm of human culture is the realm of such relative truths. It is not the realm of untruth, of evil itself; although it exists under the constant threat of evil, it is not itself evil, for it is ultimately the result of God's creation, through human creativity, and therefore good. However, unlike the new world of the kingdom of God, the old world is subject to evil and human sinning, and is therefore a world destined to pass away.

How does the Christian get along in the relative world of human culture? On the one hand, the Christian could construct an alternative culture, a "Christian" culture, side by side with the world of human culture. A Christian culture could mean Christian politics, Christian art, Christian education, Christian entertainment, a Christian style of life. The conservative churches have attempted to construct such a culture, but does the gospel of Christ attested in Holy Scripture call forth such a response? Is not the attempt to place the word "Christian" before various relative constructions—music, art, philosophy, dress—a terrible act of human pride, seeking to make divine and absolute what is in fact the very human and relative world of culture? Verses here or there may be found in the Bible to support such a view, but where in Holy Scripture is an authentic and sustained effort to construct a Christian culture of this sort?

On the other hand, the Christian can simply accept the world of culture as it is. The Christian can enjoy and pursue a religious life on the one hand, and participate without reservation in the world of culture on the other. Or, perhaps a more common solution, one can accept religion itself as another manifestation of culture, another human construction, and apply oneself to Christianity as one does to music, the arts, entertainment, and the like. The liberal churches have to some extent embraced such an alternative in one form or another. Whatever are the prevailing winds of culture then come to hold sway in the church; the Christian in these liberal churches possesses no critical norm by which to judge his or her involvement, until even the gospel and the Bible and faith itself come to flow along in the stream of relative human values.

How ought the Christian, then, to relate to the world of human culture? How is the Christian to get along in the world, as he or she lives the life of faith, hope, and love? The truth of the gospel relativizes the truths of culture in a radical way, and therefore invalidates the attempt to construct an absolute culture. Yet, the truths of culture are relative, not arbitrary; to suggest that there are no absolute values in culture is not to say that participation in culture is simply a matter of caprice or whim. How could it be so? If Jesus Christ died for the world, how could any part of that world be outside the scope of his word and work?

The answer is to be found in what the Bible calls wisdom. God promises to those who trust him not only the grace of faith, hope, and love; not only the new world of the kingdom of God, redeemed in the cross of Jesus Christ; but also the spirit of wisdom to live life in the old world which is passing away. Wisdom does not save us; only faith, hope, and love bring us into the righteousness of God. But wisdom blesses us as we seek to live in the world that is passing away.

What is wisdom? It is knowledge and understanding about the way of the world. It is a spirit of discernment about good and evil. Wisdom means the ability to relate effectively to other people, to communicate as well as to listen appropriately. Wisdom is understanding about how things work, from science and technology to economics and medicine. Wisdom is the cultivation and appreciation of beauty. It is the ability correctly to assess why things happen as they do: what motivates people, what can be changed and what cannot. Wisdom is the capacity to find and make happiness: to set limits for our work and our leisure, to respect and enjoy our friendships, to pursue pleasure and comfort within the bounds of sense. Wisdom reflects on the affairs of government: it understands politics, but it also discerns right and wrong. Wisdom is never mistaken about the surface attractiveness of power. It knows that power always corrupts, and that the exercise of force in war is usually motivated by greed and lust, seldom by concern for justice.

Wisdom is critical involvement in the world of human culture. It brings with it the skill of making choices about one's style of life and one's participation in the world. Wisdom tells me, for example, to look beneath the surface of things before I make my choices. It tells me that pride and strength, contrary to appearance, seldom make for success; that instead, it is humility and gentleness that flourish. Wisdom tells me that, despite appearances, honesty and sincerity will win over lying and manipulation. Wisdom tells me that wealth does not bring happiness, that the truly wealthy and truly successful are those who have all they need, no matter how little that is, and who give away what they do not need to those who have not. Wisdom tells me that those countries will succeed whose policies protect human rights, who protect and serve the interests of the poor

against the rich, and whose leaders are themselves subject to the rule of justice. Wisdom tells me that everyone deserves a fair wage for an honest day's work.

Wisdom is a capacity to find my way in the world, to
enjoy what it has to offer, yet not to be fooled by its
false promises. If I am wise, I am constantly learning
how to make sense of my life. Without wisdom, I
become a fool.

How do I get wisdom? Where does it come from?
Certainly the most important, and most comprehensive,
answer we can give is simply: wisdom comes from God.
"The fear of the Lord is the beginning of wisdom"
(Prov. 9:10). I can learn to find my way in the world,
coming to understand its mystery and correctly to discern its rhythms, only through the grace of God in my
mind and heart. We do not speak here about "God" in
general—is there such a thing?—but about the God
who is revealed to us as Father, Son, and Spirit, the God
who redeems us through the death of his Son on the
cross. This God offers his creatures the capacity and
skill to make their way in the world; even though the
world is passing away in light of the kingdom of God,
God does not leave us alone in this world.

Wisdom is attested for us in Holy Scripture: in the
Old Testament in books like Job, Proverbs, and Ecclesiastes, and in the New Testament in many of the parables and sayings of Jesus and in the letter of James. In
biblical texts like these it is made clear that wisdom
comes from lived experience in the presence of God.
That is to say, wisdom is not an absolute "content"
delivered once for all to believers; it is, rather, a process
of applying the truth of the known God to the relative

values of the world of human culture. Those who read faithfully the book of Proverbs, for example, know that its contents cannot be systematically arranged into a set of ethical norms or laws. Wisdom is not like that; it is not a law applied to a situation, but a direction in life derived from a situation as discerned in the light of the knowledge of God. That is not to say that wisdom is arbitrary, or an excuse for living any life that we choose. Though wisdom cannot be summarized as a convenient system of rules, it is a quality of life that adheres to all who possess it. God has made known to us through Holy Scripture just what a wise human life looks like, and also the life of a fool. If I want to be wise, and not a fool, I cannot gain wisdom by memorizing a set of rules; rather, I acquire wisdom through the experience of living life under the direction of God.

Because it is a process, and not an absolute content, there is a measure of self-determination, and therefore a pluralism, in wisdom. Because everyone has a different life experience, I must determine for myself what is the wise course to take. Not that I determine for myself as opposed to God—that would be folly—but that I determine for myself as distinguished from accepting the decisions of others. Christians will rightly differ on the choices they make in art, in politics, in recreation, in styles of life. Every Christian is offered by God the gift of wisdom, and thus undergoes the same process of acquiring it; but it is the process, and the God who directs it, that are constant, not the content of the choices that are made. These can vary, even as they often do in Holy Scripture. The point here, as Luther said, is that God alone is master of the conscience. Those who allow others to legislate for them the "Christian" approach to art, or politics, or culture generally are inviting in a competitor to the one true God; and those who would legislate for others such answers are the teachers of fools.

What is the relation between faith, hope, and love on the one hand, and wisdom on the other? Wisdom is the process of applying faith, hope, and love to the old world that is passing away. Through wisdom, I live out my faith, hope, and love in the world of human culture. In other words, the Christian life not only gives me a new citizenship in the kingdom of God, and therefore a new way of relating to God, to my neighbor, and in these relations a new self; the Christian life also gives me a new way of relating to the world of culture. That is to become wise in my dealings with the world, wise in the way that God gives me to be wise.

Because my citizenship has been transferred to a new world, the coming kingdom of God, there is inevitably a measure of tension in my dealings with the old world. Insofar as the old world lives under the threat of sin and evil, I must be prepared at times, in wisdom, simply to say no. When culture contributes to injustice, to violence, to hatred, to neglect of the poor and outcast, to greed, I can only take my stand against culture. I must do so no matter what the cost to me personally. Indeed, it is a measure of the authenticity of my faith that I must at times say no, and that indeed the world will say no to me.

Fortunately, the world of human culture is not always evil. Though relative, there is at times a measure of truth, of beauty, of excellence, of brilliance, in the achievements of human beings. Why should that not be so? Although we are all sinners to the very core, we are still God's creatures. While God has provided a new kingdom ruled by love and forgiveness, he continues to uphold and sustain the passing world. Will it not therefore show some signs of his bounty? To be sure, when the Christian says yes to some aspect of human culture—when, for example, he or she joins a political campaign working for greater justice, or celebrates an artistic movement, or enjoys a style of music—that yes is always relative; it accepts what culture has to offer without mistaking it for something more. Nevertheless, it is a yes.

Whether I say yes or no to this or that aspect of the human culture of the present, as a Christian I always know that my wisdom flourishes only within the limits of my faith, just as this world stands under the sign of the cross as the victory of Jesus Christ over the world. When wisdom outgrows faith it becomes folly; it shares in the folly of the world in its pride and rebellion against God. When I accept the limits of wisdom, I am free to enjoy whatever is to be enjoyed in the world of culture. This world does not offer me redemption, or at least I must refuse to find it there when it is offered. But precisely because I have been redeemed by God, I am free to accept the world for what it is. The Christian is in a unique position to appreciate what the world has to offer; as strange as it sounds, the wise Christian may be the world's last humanist.

The Gospel and the Future

As INDIVIDUAL Christians, as members of the body of Christ, and as participants in the culture of our time, we cannot help wondering where history is going. What does the future hold for us individually and for the world as a whole? We can speak of the world as a whole in a way that has seldom been possible in human history, for, while national histories continue, somehow the destiny of the peoples of the world seems intricately linked. What happens in New York matters in Tokyo; what happens in Johannesburg is connected with events in Berlin; events in Moscow affect life in San Salvador. History is no longer a collection of independent time lines like strands in a rope; it is a fabric of interwoven material whose unity makes it appear almost seamless. Thus, we can now meaningfully ask in a way that was not previously possible: Where is history going?

The gospel proclaims that the world has been redeemed by God through the life, death, and resurrection of Jesus Christ; that, in him, God has accomplished for us a relationship between God and humanity, a relationship so certain and so vital that it means an entirely new world. It is a world in which sin is forgiven, sickness is healed, oppression is overthrown, and death itself is dead. It is a world in which humanity, and indeed all that exists, reaches final, definitive fulfillment.

Yet as we stand at the threshold of the third millennium after Christ, we must ask: Where is this new world? Can it be seen by looking back over history? Is it concealed in the pages of the story of civilization? No; for when, as Christians, we look backward over time, we see the cross of Jesus Christ. We see the life of this one individual, Jesus Christ, who proclaimed the coming of the kingdom, was delivered over to be crucified, and on the third day was raised from the dead.

The perspective of two millennia of history gives no more perspective to this event than was had the day after it occurred, for it is not an event made meaningful by the history in which it is embedded, but an event that gives meaning to that history.

What meaning does it give to that history? It tells us that history is passing—not simply the truism that history is the story of events that have already occurred, but the truth that the time of history is passing away in the coming kingdom of God. To view our time in the shadow of the cross means to see the kingdom of God in the life, death, and resurrection of Jesus Christ as more real than nations, than culture, than the rise and fall of entire civilizations. That does not mean that history is meaningless, but it does mean that all history stands radically under the sign of the cross.

There are some who point to "anticipations of the kingdom" in the events of the world. Where the sick are healed, prisoners are set free, the naked are clothed, the oppressed are liberated, it is said that the kingdom of God has in a preliminary way begun to grow stronger; that what was inaugurated by Jesus can and will expand in power and scope until it embraces the whole world. To be sure, who cannot be grateful to God when such things occur? Are they not certainly the signs of God's blessing and presence in human life? Yet, do we really do the gospel justice when we speak of "anticipations of the kingdom"? Who can look around in the past and present of human history and really see the kingdom of God as Jesus proclaimed it? Both in our own hearts and in our witness to others, do we not lose hope when we try to find the kingdom of God in the past and present of world events? The kingdom of God is with us, but not as the inner meaning of world history; it is with us because *he* is with us, Jesus Christ, who died and rose again for our sake and is seated at the right hand of the throne of God. He is the kingdom of God; his rule is not only its anticipation, but its reality. When Christians look back, they see Jesus only (see Mark 9:8).

If we cannot look back over time to give meaning to history, and to our time and our future, can we look ahead? Can we predict the future, and then give our own time meaning and perspective? Is the Christian in any unique position to know the content of the future? For some, so-called "biblical prophecy" amounts to just such a blueprint for the prediction of the future. The language of the Bible that bears witness to the end of the age and the coming of the kingdom is then used supposedly to foretell the rise and fall of nations, the destiny of peoples and places, the fortune of the economic system, and so forth. However earnest the endeavor to interpret biblical texts as prophetic predictions, the effort as a whole must fail, for the biblical texts do not predict the future of our time, but attest the coming of a new time. They are not predictions, but true prophecy; not futurology, but eschatology; they do not give details about the future as if they are tomorrow's newspaper, but testify to the promise of God concerning his kingdom because they are the word of God.

For others, the eschatological language of the New Testament is simply an outmoded worldview, the mythological language of ancient culture. Its usefulness came to an end when the expected return of Christ was delayed more than one generation. At best, it must be reinterpreted existentially (as in Bultmann); at worst, it must be discarded altogether (as in Harnack). Now, while the eschatology of the Bible cannot be used to predict the future, neither can it be dismissed as an outmoded conceptuality. For it is not a "conceptuality," not the "vehicle" containing the "message" of the early church; it *is* the message of Jesus himself and of his witnesses.

What is that message? How does it relate to our future? A text here will help: Jesus said, "This generation will not pass away until all things have taken place" (Luke 21:32). We ask: Which generation? Was it the first generation? Or the next generation after his death? Or some succeeding generation? The answer to these questions does not lie in the attempt historically to fix the referent of these words, or to reconstruct the social context of their transmission and use. The answer lies in the simple recognition that it is our generation that now reads these words; our generation that now hears in them the voice of Jesus Christ laying claim to our lives and hearts. Not because we can predict the future, but because Jesus himself promises his coming must we live our lives with the hope that ours is the last generation before the passing of our age and the dawning of the new world of the kingdom of God. We must live our lives in preparation for the kingdom of God. If we could predict it, it would no longer be what the Bible describes it to be: sudden and unexpected. Precisely because it is unexpected, we must expect it at any time, and indeed in our time.

What does this mean for our lives? A feverish attempt to straighten things out before he arrives? No, for Jesus will himself straighten things out when he arrives. It means, rather, a sense for just how relative are the things of our world—not that they are worthless, but that they are soon to pass away. It means adopting a system of priorities that recognizes the endurance of faith, hope, and love, especially love, and the impermanence of everything else. Everything else? Yes indeed; for the future of the world is not capitalist or socialist; not American or Russian, European or Asian or African; it is not democratic or monarchical or tyrannical; it will not trade in the coin of any nation, nor fly any flags whatsoever. The future of the world is the new world of God in Jesus Christ, who has come for our forgiveness and will come for our deliverance. He will come with his peace, his righteousness, his justice, his mercy. And because he died and rose to redeem our lives, he will come to gather us together for eternal life in his kingdom. Jesus is Lord!

Biblical Texts for Consideration

The Gospel in the Church

Matthew 5:14–16
Matthew 16:13–20
Matthew 28:16–20
Acts 2
1 Corinthians 12
Galatians 3:23–29
Ephesians 4:1–16
Colossians 3:1–17

The Gospel and Human Culture

Proverbs 10–24
Ecclesiastes
James 1–2

The Gospel and the Future

Matthew 24
Mark 13
Luke 21

NOTES

Chapter 1

1. I use the terms "conservative" and "liberal" rather loosely here to describe the obvious split in contemporary North American Christianity. These terms have been used in other contexts for different purposes. I do not mean to suggest that every Christian, or church, is either conservative or liberal. I only wish to invite my readers to struggle with the broad division in North American Christianity and perhaps, in the face of that struggle, to find a fresh theological witness.

2. Another alternative is arguably present in the various liberation theologies, in which the suffering of oppression and the ideological critique of religion provide theology and the church with a different insight into Christian faith. I nevertheless would argue that in North America, at least, liberation theology tends to function as an extension of the basic paradigm of modern, liberal Christianity.

3. Indeed, because it uses the techniques of modern theology for its critique—in particular the self-constituting and self-validating nature of human experience—liberation theology is the *reductio ad absurdum* of liberalism. Theology, to paraphrase Feuerbach, has become ideology.

4. I shall here use the term "modern" theology very loosely to describe the basic paradigm of theology in the more liberal churches, and the term "fundamentalist" theology to describe the basic paradigm in the more conservative churches. These terms are used differently in other contexts. My point here is not to exhaust the possibilities, nor to pigeonhole anyone. I am trying to describe a basic division in theology which seems to override in importance and strength the many theological options available, and furthermore, arguing that coming to grips with this basic division is crucial.

5. When I speak here, and elsewhere, of "literalism" in the interpretation of the Bible, I mean overly restrictive attention to the verbal sense of the text, in abstraction from its living content. Similarly, when I speak of "interpretation" I mean the need for human response to the text in the broadest sense. In its strategy of defense against modern theology, fundamentalism seems to lose its sense of the living content of the text, at the same time as it eliminates the need for human response. What I am arguing for is what the reformers called the *sensus literalis*—the verbal sense in living unity with the subject matter of the text calling each new generation to fresh response.

6. The point is not to create a tension between faithfulness to the gospel and relevance to our world. The enormous theological challenge to us today is to work toward a Christian witness that is at the same time faithful and relevant. Scripture itself seems to call forth such a witness.

7. Traditional-historical work on the canon of scripture, both Old and New Testaments, has shown to what extent the traditions were always witness rather than source. In that crucial sense, a theological reading of the text is preeminently historical.

Chapter 2

1. Like many theologians, I sometimes in this book use the name God in the sense of God the Father and sometimes in the sense of the Godhead—Father, Son, and Spirit. It is hoped that the context will make clear the meaning.

2. I shall, throughout this book, use the present tense as well as the past tense in reflecting theologically on Jesus Christ in the Gospel witness. The point is not to separate "history" from "story"; the Gospels are clearly a testimony to true history. The point, rather, is to hear the biblical narrative in all its immediacy, in its unique combination of truth and meaning in bearing witness to the earthly life of Jesus.

3. The Bible is well aware of the fact that the gift of God's name can be misused to abuse others, especially the vulnerable. Such indeed is the demonic nature of sin; it twists and distorts the very gifts of God for our salvation. But the answer is not to reject the gifts, or the name of the gift giver. Indeed, in his name is our only salvation.

4. It should be noted that I have here accepted the customary critique of the conceptuality of the ancient church. I do not, however, accept the customary critique of the *witness* of the early church, but rather affirm the confession of faith that was made using this conceptuality. Failure to read classical theology confessionally not only leads to mishearing its witness, it is moreover not historically persuasive.

Chapter 5

1. Let me summarize briefly. By the new world of God, or the coming kingdom of God, I mean the mysterious rule of Jesus Christ. As the risen Lord and Savior, his rule is already public and actual throughout the world, but it can be seen only by the eyes of faith. Indeed, it is real, but real in the concealment of Word and sacrament, real in the secret work of the Spirit in ruling the hearts of the people of God. Moreover, it grows in secret through the sovereign

191

grace of God, until that day—the day for which we wait—when Christ shall be manifest to all in his glory.

2. It is perhaps worth noting here that ideological perspectives on involvement with others depend upon the illusion of a world order of justice and peace which I, along with others, can create. Ideologies therefore deny the reality and extent of sin. And when reality comes to contradict the ideology, the inevitable mechanism is to look for victims to blame. "And many false prophets will arise and lead many astray. And because of the increase of lawlessness, the love of many will grow cold" (Matt. 24:11–12).

The difference between Christian faith and an ideology is in Christ himself. An ideology needs adherents in order to survive; it will therefore inevitably exact its price. Jesus Christ does not need us in order to live. He wants to be with us simply because he loves us; he paid the price for us. (See John 10:1–18.)

Chapter 6

1. It seems to me that there are four options here. First, that the boundaries of human life are untouched by the gospel. Second, that the boundaries of human life are transcended and transformed by the gospel. Third, that the boundaries are eliminated through the concept of undifferentiated *humanitas*. Fourth, that the boundaries are eliminated through ideological struggle. I am convinced that scripture supports the second option.